PRICE GUIDE

to Packers Memorabilia

John Carpentier

Published by

 **krause**
publications

700 E. State Street • Iola, WI 54990-0001
Telephone: 715/445-2214

Please call or write for our free catalog of publications.
Our toll-free number to place an order or obtain a free catalog is 800-258-0929 or please use
our regular business telephone 715-445-2214 for editorial comment and further information.

Library of Congress Catalog Number: 97-80607
ISBN: 0-87341-572-8

Printed in the United States of America

Dedication

Green Bay Packers fans are the greatest football fans in the world. Many people around the country support the Packers because they love a small town in Wisconsin with fans who are loyal all the time—not just when the team is winning. The frozen tundra of Lambeau Field is sacred ground to Packers fans. I dedicate this book to the Packers greats of yesteryear: Curly Lambeau, Don Hutson, Vince Lombardi and the hundreds of others that played football for the love of the game.

—John Carpentier

Table of Contents

Introduction

About This Guide

"What is it worth?" That's a question I hear often when it comes to Green Bay Packers memorabilia. Hopefully this book, *Price Guide to Packers Memorabilia*, will help answer many of those questions, whether you're a fan of Curly Lambeau and Don Hutson, Bart Starr and Paul Hornung or Brett Favre and Reggie White...and all Packers in-between.

This guide covers all types of different Packers items—40 categories in all—from the common to the obscure. Each chapter contains an introduction that explains what the items are, along with collecting tips and other important details. Following this introductory information are current value ranges for the various items.

The values listed in this book are prices at which you could expect dealers to sell these items (retail price), not the price a dealer would pay for them. Dealers will generally pay from 30% to 70% of the retail price, depending on the current demand for the item. The more in-demand the item is, the more a dealer will be willing to pay. Many of the chapters have pictures showing specific items and their values.

Price guides are designed to assist collectors in establishing a fair price for their items. Many factors go into determining an item's value. Age, condition, demand and, most important, personal attachment, all contribute to establishing value. For example, a Lynn Dickey autograph you got in person in the 1980s probably has a lot more value to you personally than it would on the open market.

Many trends have come and gone in the collectibles field. Today, Baby Boomers are buying back many items they had in their youth. One of the most popular items are the bobbing head dolls from the 1960s. Originally costing about $1, they can now cost up to several hundred dollars! The same is true for the board games that were made featuring the Packers in the 1960s and 1970s.

Numerous items are now being made as collectibles. Most of these collectible items will seldom be thrown away. Remember that many of today's valuable collectibles were thrown out or given away because most people didn't think they would become valuable (like baseball cards). If you purchase an expensive new collectible item today, it may not go up in value. Because of this, I advise people to collect items because they like them. That way, if the item goes up in value, that's great; if it doesn't, then you still have something you like. If you are buying items for investment purposes, find items that are unique and in top condition. Avoid items that are in poor condition, massed-produced or are common.

People collect for a variety of reasons. With many Packers fans, it's a part of you that goes back to your childhood. Many Packers fans have parents, grandparents and even great-grandparents who followed the Pack. While the Packers have historically had a very strong following, the 1997 Super Bowl win has taken the interest level for Packers memorabilia another step or two higher.

If I can help you in any way with questions you have regarding the buying or selling of any Green Bay Packers memorabilia, please drop me a line or give me a call at Packer City Antiques, P.O. Box 866, Green Bay, WI 54304; phone (920) 490-1095.

Where to Find Packers Items

Green Bay Packers items are most plentiful in the Midwest, most notably in Wisconsin and the Green Bay area. This makes a lot of sense, since this is the location of the Packers and many Packers items were issued on a regional basis. You can, however, find Packers items outside this region, as many items were sold nationally. Sports, antique and toy dealers in Wisconsin and the Midwest are good sources to find Packers memorabilia. Shops, shows, flea markets and garage sales are all good places to locate Packers items. And, of course, Packer City Antiques, the largest buyer and seller of old Packers memorabilia in the country.

Two good magazines to find football cards and memorabilia for sale are *Sports Collectors Digest* and *Sports Cards. Toy Shop* magazine has dealers who sell Packers games and other Packers toys. The huge reference book, *1998 Standard Catalog of Football Cards*, is a must if you are a serious football card collector. This book contains 400 pages, 800 photos, 80,000 card values and listings for all cards from 1894 to the present. These publications can be ordered from Krause Publications, 700 E. State St., Iola, WI 54990-0001, 800-258-0929.

If you'd like to view many historical Packers items, plan a trip to the Green Bay Packers Hall of Fame in Green Bay. Many say the Packers Hall of Fame might be better than the Pro Football Hall of Fame in Canton, Ohio.

Thanks to...

Photographer Ross Hubbard from Krause Publications who spent two days at my shop in Green Bay shooting the photos of the items you see in this guide, as well as the cover photo. Also, thanks to Jason Stonelake from Krause Publications who assembled the information in the trading cards section and to Stacy Bloch and Jon Stein who designed the black-and-white and color sections, respectively. Last, but certainly not least, I would like to thank my wife, Lisa, and stepson, Dan, who helped make this book possible.

Chapter 1

Ashtrays

Ashtrays are found in a variety of shapes and sizes. Ashtrays from the 1930s and 1940s are not common finds. There were many ashtrays made in the 1960s. In 1961, an ashtray in the shape of Lambeau Field had a small removable player figurine at the top of it. Some of the most popular ashtrays are the "Sneezer" ashtrays, featuring the players' and coaches' facsimile signatures from Sneezer's Snack Shop (they are round, green and gold and were made from 1959-1961). The newspaper-headline ashtrays from the 1960s are also becoming valuable. Championship and Super Bowl ashtrays are in demand and escalating in price. Make sure to check for chips, cracks and wear that can detract from the value.

Age	*Price Range*	
1920s (very rare)	75.00	200.00
1930s	50.00	150.00
1940s	35.00	125.00
1950s	25.00	100.00
1960s	15.00	95.00
1970s	8.00	50.00
1980s	4.00	25.00
1990s	2.00	20.00

12 World Championships

With 12 world championships, the Packers have won more than any other team in NFL history. The Chicago Bears have won nine; the New York Giants won six; the Dallas Cowboys, San Francisco 49ers and Washington Redskins won five each; and the Detroit Lions and Cleveland Browns won four apiece. The Packers are the only team to win three straight championships, having accomplished this twice. Here are the championship years: 1929, 1930, 1931, 1936, 1939, 1944, 1961, 1962, 1965, 1966, 1967, 1996.

1960, "Sneezer's Snack Shop" ashtray, green & gold, facsimile autographs of team and coaches ($45-$95).

1961 newspaper headline ashtray, b&w ($30-$60).

1965 newspaper headline ashtray, green and white ($25-$55).

1970s, clear glass, "Were Backers" ashtray ($10-$20).

Chapter 2

Autographs—Coaches, Players & Team

Collecting autographs can be difficult. Many signed items today come with certificates of authenticity that sometimes do not include the age or origin of a signature. Whenever possible, try to find autographs that have as much information as possible. Hand-written documents are better than printed certificates. Many factors determine an autograph's price. Staining, fading, smearing and other damage can reduce the value of an autograph. The item that a signature is on can be worth more than the signature itself. Autograph shows did not evolve until the 1970s. Older signed items from the 1920s to the 1960s are difficult to obtain.

The rise in autograph values has brought a large amount of modern signed

1942 team photo, 11" x 14", b&w, signed by entire team and coaches—Lambeau, Hutson, etc. ($500-$1,250).

items. Limited edition prints, mini-helmets, jerseys and footballs are available in abundance. The best way to assure that an autograph is authentic is to obtain it in person. If that is not possible, try to use the most reliable source possible.

Be careful when purchasing the newer white-panel footballs made for autographing. Some of the inks used in the marker pens fade or absorb into the ball. If you are getting a signature on a ball, use a Sharpie or a paint pen. Be careful when handling signed items. Secure them in a frame, case, bag, or something that will allow it to be handled without touching the signature. The oils in our skin, plus any substances left on the fingers, can damage signatures.

1992 Packer team-issued helmet, used, signed by several members of the 1993 team—Favre, Detmer, Brooks, etc. ($500-$750); same helmet unsigned ($75-$200).

One of the most confusing areas of autographs is telling the difference between a printed or stamped signature and a real one. Authentic team signed footballs have random signatures. Stamped footballs usually have evenly spaced signatures that are very straight across. Most stamped footballs are done in a black ink. When a football was signed with different colored pens, it is usually authentic. Most of the stamped footballs are signed in rows. If players are missing or if other persons besides players and coaches have signed on a football, it is usually authentic.

Most black-and-white signed photographs from the 1960s to the 1990s (given out by the team) had printed signatures. The player signed an original photo and then the team copied them.

The prices below are for individual signatures of Packers head coaches, players and team-signed items from 1921 to the present. The price ranges depend on the condition of the signature(s) and the item it is signed on.

Head Coach/Years with Packers   *Price Range*

Head Coach/Years with Packers	Low	High
Earl "Curly" Lambeau, (HOF), 1921-49	200.00	500.00
Gene Ronzani, 1950-53	15.00	50.00
Lisle Blackbourn, 1954-57	12.00	40.00
Ray "Scooter" McLean, 1958	10.00	35.00

Packer check, front, 4/6/59, made out to William "Max" McGee, signed by Lombardi ($250-$400).

Packer check, back, 4/6/59, endorsed by McGee ($250-$400).

Season Scoring Leaders (no TDs)

1. Chester Marcol, 128
2. Chris Jacke, 128
3. Jan Stenerud, 115
4. Chris Jacke, 114
5. Chris Jacke, 108

Packer check, front, 7/18/60, made out to Vince Lombardi/endorsed by Lombardi, rare ($450-$750).

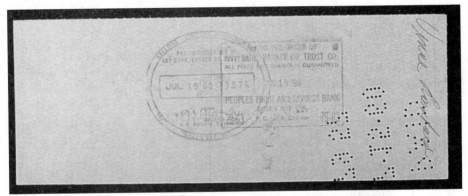

Packer check, back, 7/18/60, endorsed by Lombardi, rare ($450-$750).

Single Season Scoring Leaders

1. Paul Hornung, 176 points (15 touchdowns, 41 extra points, 15 field goals)
2. Paul Hornung, 146 (10 touchdowns, 41 extra points, 15 field goals)
3. Don Hutson, 138 (17 touchdowns, 33 extra points, one field goal)

Vince Lombardi, (HOF), 1959-67 ....100.00   300.00
Phil Bengston, 1968-70...10.00   35.00
Dan Devine, 1971-74 ....10.00   25.00
Bart Starr, (HOF), 1975-83 ....25.00   55.00
Forrest Gregg, (HOF), 1984-84 ....12.00   30.00
Lindy Infante, 1988-91 ....10.00   25.00
Mike Holmgren, 1992-97..15.00   45.00

A

Player/Position/College/Years with Packers   *Price Range*

Aberson, Cliff, (B), no college, 1946......................................10.00   30.00
Abrams, Nate, (E), no college, 1921.....................................20.00   75.00
Abramson, George, (T), Minnesota, 1925 ....15.00   45.00
Acks, Ron, (LB), Arizona State, 1974-76..............................3.00   15.00
Adams, Chet, (T), Ohio State, 1942-43 ....10.00   30.00
Adderley, Herb, (B), Michigan State, (HOF), 1961-69 ....15.00   35.00
Adkins, Bob, (B), Marshall, 1940-41, 1945-46 ....10.00   25.00
Affholter, Erik, (WR), USC, 1991 ....3.00   10.00
Afflis, Dick "The Bruiser," (G), Nevada, 1951-55 ....20.00   50.00
Agajanian, Ben, (K), New Mexico, 1961 ....5.00   20.00
Albrecht, Art, (T), Wisconsin, 1941 ....10.00   25.00
Aldrige, Ben, (B), Oklahoma A&M, 1953 ....5.00   20.00
Aldrige, Lionel, (DE), Utah State, 1963-71 ....8.00   20.00
Allerman, Kurt, (LB), Penn State, 1980-81 ....3.00   15.00
Amundsen, Norm, (G), Wisconsin, 1957................................8.00   25.00
Amsler, Marty, (DE), Evansville, 1970 ....3.00   10.00
Anderson, Aric, (LB), Millikin, 1970 ....3.00   10.00
Anderson, Bill, (E), Tennessee, 1965-66 ....8.00   20.00
Anderson, Donny, (B), Texas Tech, 1966-71 ....10.00   25.00
Anderson, John, (LB), Michigan, 1978-89 ....5.00   15.00
Anderson, Vickey Ray, (FB), Oklahoma, 1980.......................3.00   10.00
Ane, Charlie, (C), Michigan State, 1981................................3.00   10.00
Apsit, Marger, (B), USC, 1932 ....10.00   30.00
Archambeua, Lester, (DE), Stanford, 1990-92 ....3.00   10.00
Ard, Billy, (G/T), Wake Forest, 1989-91...............................3.00   10.00

Player/Position/College/Years with Packers	Price	Range
Ariery, Mike, (T), San Diego State, 1989	3.00	10.00
Arthur, Mike, (C), Texas A&M, 1995	3.00	10.00
Ashmore, Roger, (T), Gonzaga, 1928-29	15.00	45.00
Askson, Bert, (TE), Texas Southern, 1975-77	4.00	12.00
Atkins, Steve, (B), Maryland, 1979-81	3.00	10.00
Auer, Todd, (LB), Western Illinois, 1987	3.00	10.00
Austin, Hise, (DB), Prairie View A&M, 1973	4.00	12.00
Avery, Steve, (FB), Northern Michigan, 1991	3.00	10.00
Aydelette, Buddy, (T), Alabama, 1980-81	3.00	10.00

B

	Price	Range
Bailey, Byron, (B), Washington State, 1953	8.00	25.00
Bain, Bill, (T), USC, 1975	4.00	12.00
Baker, Frank, (E), Northwestern, 1931	15.00	40.00
Baker, Roy, (B), USC, 1928-29	15.00	45.00
Balaz, Frank, (B), Iowa, 1939-41	10.00	35.00
Baldwin, Al, (E), Arkansas, 1950	10.00	25.00
Banet, Herb, (B), Manchester, 1937	10.00	35.00
Barber, Bob, (DE), Gramling, 1976-79	3.00	12.00
Barnes, Emery, (E), Oregon, 1956	10.00	25.00
Barnes, Gary, (E), Clemson, 1962-63	5.00	25.00
Barnett, Solon, (T), Baylor, 1945-46	10.00	30.00
Barragar, Nate, (C), USC, 1931-35	15.00	35.00
Barrett, Jan, (E), Fresno State, 1963	5.00	15.00
Barrie, Sebastian, (DE), Liberty University, 1992	3.00	10.00
Barry, Al, (G), USC, 1954-57	10.00	30.00
Barry, Norm, (B), Notre Dame, 1921	15.00	75.00
Barton, Don, (B), Texas, 1953	8.00	20.00
Bartum, Mike, (TE), Marshall, 1995	3.00	10.00
Barzilauskas, Carl, (DT), Indiana, 1979-79	4.00	12.00
Basing, Myrt, (B), Lawrence, 1923-27	20.00	60.00
Basinger, Mike, (DE), Cal-Riverside, 1974	4.00	12.00
Baxter, Lloyd, (T), Southern Methodist, 1948	5.00	25.00
Beach, Sanjay, (WR), Colorado State, 1992	3.00	10.00
Beasley, John, (B), South Dakota, 1924	20.00	60.00

Player/Position/College/Years with Packers		Price Range
Beck, Ken, (T), Texas A&M, 1959-60	8.00	20.00
Becker, Wayland, (E), Marquette, 1936-38	10.00	40.00
Beekley, Bruce, (LB), Oregon, 1980	3.00	10.00
Bell, Albert, (WR), Alabama, 1988	3.00	10.00
Bell, Ed, (G), Indiana, 1947-49	5.00	25.00
Bennett, Earl, (G), Hardin-Simmons, 1946	5.00	25.00
Bennett, Edgar, (RB), Florida State, 1992-	10.00	25.00
Bennett, Tony, (LB), Mississippi, 1990-93	5.00	15.00
Berenezy, Paul, (T), Fordham, 1942-44	8.00	30.00
Berrang, Ed, (E), Villanova, 1952	5.00	20.00
Berry, Connie, (E), North Carolina State, 1940	10.00	30.00
Berry, Ed, (DB), Utah State, 1986	3.00	10.00
Bettencourt, Larry, (C), St. Mary's, 1933	15.00	45.00
Bettis, Tom, (LB), Purdue, 1955-61	10.00	25.00
Beverly, David, (P), Auburn, 1975-80	5.00	12.00
Bilda, Dick, (B), Marquette, 1944	8.00	30.00
Billups, Lewis, (CB), North Alabama, 1992	3.00	10.00
Biolo, John, (G), Lake Forest, 1939	15.00	45.00
Birney, Tom, (K), Michigan State, 1979-80	5.00	20.00
Blaine, Ed, (G), Missouri, 1962	8.00	20.00
Bland, Carl, (WR), Virginia Union, 1989-90	3.00	10.00
Bloodgood, El, (B), Nebraska, 1930	15.00	45.00
Boedeker, Bill, (B), Kalamazoo, 1950	5.00	20.00
Boerio, Chuck, (LB), Illinois, 1952	5.00	20.00
Bolton, Scott, (WR), Auburn, 1988	3.00	10.00
Bone, Warran, (LB), Texas Southern, 1987	3.00	10.00
Bookout, Billy, (B), Austin, 1955-56	5.00	20.00
Boone, J.R., (B), Tulsa, 1953	5.00	20.00
Borak, Fritz, (E), Crieghton, 1938	15.00	30.00
Borden, Nate, (E), Indiana, 1955-59	5.00	20.00
Borgognone, Dirk, (K), Pacific, 1955	3.00	10.00
Bowdoin, Jim, (G), Alabama, 1928-32	20.00	60.00
Bowman, Ken, (C), Wisconsin, 1964-73	10.00	25.00
Boyarski, Jerry, (NT), Pittsburgh, 1986-89	3.00	10.00
Boyd, Elmo, (WR), Eastern Kentucky, 1978	4.00	10.00
Boyd, Greg, (DE), San Diego State, 1983	3.00	10.00

Player/Position/College/Years with Packers	_Price Range_	
Bracken, Don, (P), Michigan, 1985-90	4.00	10.00
Brackens, Charlie, (B), Prairie View A&M, 1955	5.00	20.00
Bradley, Dave, (G), Penn State, 1969-71	5.00	12.00
Brady, Jeff, (LB), Kentucky, 1992	3.00	10.00
Braggs, Byron, (DT), Alabama, 1981-83	3.00	10.00
Branstetter, Kent, (G/T), Houston, 1973	4.00	12.00
Bradkowski, Zeke, (QB), Georgia, 1963-68, 1971	10.00	25.00
Bray, Ray, (G), Western Michigan, 1952	5.00	20.00
Breen, Jene, (LB), Virginia Tech, 1964	5.00	20.00
Brennan, John, (G), Michigan, 1939	15.00	40.00
Brock, Charlie, (C), Nebraska, 1939-47	15.00	30.00
Brock, Lou, (B), Purdue, 1940-45	10.00	45.00
Brock, Matt, (DE/DT), Oregon, 1989-94	3.00	10.00
Brockington, John, (RB), Ohio State, 1971-77	10.00	20.00
Brooks, Robert, (WR), South Carolina, 1992-	10.00	25.00
Broussard, Steve, (P), Southern Miss, 1975	4.00	10.00
Brown, Aaron, (DE), Minnesota, 1973-74	4.00	10.00
Brown, Allen, (E), Mississippi, 1966-67	10.00	20.00
Brown, Bill, (G), Arkansas, 1953-56	5.00	20.00
Brown, Bob, (DT), Arkansas AM&N, 1966-73	10.00	20.00
Brown, Carlos, (QB), Pacific (Actor), 1975-76	10.00	30.00
Brown, Dave, (CB), Michigan, 1987-89	3.00	10.00
Brown, Gary, (T), Georgia Tech, 1994-96	5.00	15.00
Brown, Gilbert, (DT), Kansas, 1993-	10.00	25.00
Brown, Ken, (C), New Mexico, 1980	3.00	10.00
Brown, Robert, (LB/DE), Virginia Tech, 1982-92	4.00	10.00
Brown, Tim, (B), Ball State, 1959	8.00	20.00
Brown, Tom, (HB), Maryland, 1964-68	10.00	20.00
Browner, Ross, (NT), Notre Dame, 1987	3.00	10.00
Bruder, Hank, (B), Northwestern, 1931-39	15.00	45.00
Brunell, Mark, (QB), Washington, 1993-94	10.00	30.00
Bucchianeri, Mike, (G), Indiana, 1941, 1944-45	10.00	30.00
Bucchnon, Willie, (DB), San Diego State, 1972-78	5.00	15.00
Buck, Cub, (T), Wisconsin, 1921-25	25.00	75.00
Buckley, Terrell, (CB), Florida State, 1992-94	5.00	15.00
Buhler, Larry, (B), Minnesota, 1939-41	10.00	30.00

Player/Position/College/Years with Packers	*Price Range*	
Buland, Walt, (T), no college, 1924	20.00	45.00
Bullough, Hank, (G), Michigan State, 1955, 1958	10.00	30.00
Bultman, Art, (C), Marquette, 1932-34	10.00	30.00
Burgess, Ronny, (DB), Wake Forest, 1985	3.00	10.00
Burnette, Reggie, (LB), Houston, 1991	3.00	10.00
Burris, Paul, (G), Oklahoma, 1949-51	8.00	20.00
Burrow, Curtis, (K), Central Arkansas, 1988	3.00	10.00
Burrow, Jim, (DB), Nebraska, 1976	4.00	10.00
Bush, Blair, (C), Washington, 1989-91	3.00	10.00
Butler, Bill, (B), Chattanooga, 1959	8.00	20.00
Butler, Frank, (C), Michigan State, 1934-36, 1938	10.00	30.00
Butler, LeRoy, (CB/S), Florida State, 1990-	10.00	25.00

C

Cabral, Brian, (LB), Colorado, 1980	3.00	10.00
Cade, Mossy, (DB), Texas, 1985-86	3.00	8.00
Caffey, Lee Roy, (LB), Texas A&M, 1964-69	10.00	25.00
Cahoon, Ivan, (T), Gonzaga, 1926-29	20.00	50.00
Caldwell, David, (NT), Texas Christian, 1987	3.00	10.00
Campbell, Rich, (QB), California, 1981-84	4.00	10.00
Campen, James, (C), Tulane, 1989-93	3.00	10.00
Canadeo, Tony, (B), Gonzaga, (HOF), 1941-44, 1946-52	15.00	35.00
Cannava, Al, (B), Cincinnati, 1950	10.00	25.00
Cannon, Mark, (C), Texas-Arlington, 1985-89	3.00	10.00
Capp, Dick, (LB), Boston College, 1967	10.00	25.00
Capuzzi, Jim, (B), Cincinnati, 1955-56	10.00	25.00
Carey, Joe, (G), no college, 1921	20.00	75.00
Carlson, Dean, (QB), Iowa State, 1974	4.00	10.00
Carmichael, Al, (B), USC, 1953-58	10.00	25.00
Carpenter, Lew, (B), Arkansas, 1959-63	10.00	25.00
Carr, Fred, (LB), Texas-El-Paso, 1968-77	8.00	20.00
Carreker, Alphonso, (DE), Florida State, 1984-88	3.00	10.00
Carroll, Leo, (DE), San Diego State, 1968	8.00	20.00
Carruth, Paul Ott, (RB), Alabama, 1986-88	4.00	10.00
Carter, Carl, (CB), Texas Tech, 1992	3.00	10.00

Player/Position/College/Years with Packers	Price Range	
Carter, Jim, (LB), Minnesota, 1970-78	5.00	12.00
Carter, Joe, (E), Southern Methodist, 1942	10.00	35.00
Carter, Mike, (WR), Sacramento State, 1970-71	4.00	12.00
Casper, Charley, (B), Texas Christian, 1934	15.00	40.00
Cassidy, Ron, (WR), Utah State, 1979-81, 1983-84	4.00	12.00
Cecil, Chuck, (S), Arizona, 1988-92	4.00	12.00
Chandler, Don, (K), Florida, 1965-67	10.00	25.00
Cheek, Louis, (T), Texas A&M, 1991	3.00	10.00
Cherry, Bill, (C), Middle Tennessee State, 1986-87	3.00	10.00
Chelsey, Francis, (LB), Wyoming, 1978	3.00	10.00
Cheyunski, Jim, (LB), Syracuse, 1977	3.00	10.00
Childs, Henry, (TE), Kansas State, 1984	3.00	10.00
Chmura, Mark, (TE), Boston College, 1993-	10.00	25.00
Choate, Putt, (LB), Nebraska, 1964-65	10.00	25.00
Christman, Paul, (B), Missouri, 1950	8.00	20.00
Cifelli, Gus, (T), Notre Dame, 1953	8.00	20.00
Cifers, Bob, (B), Tennessee, 1949	8.00	20.00
Clancy, Jack, (WR), Michigan, 1970	4.00	12.00
Clanton, Chuck, (DB), Auburn, 1985	3.00	10.00
Clark, Allan, (RB), Northern Arizona, 1982	3.00	10.00
Clark, Greg, (LB), Arizona State, 1991	3.00	10.00
Clark, Jessie, (FB), Arkansas, 1983-87	4.00	12.00
Clark, Vinnie, (CB), Ohio State, 1991-92	4.00	12.00
Clavelle, Shannon, (DE), Colorado, 1995	4.00	12.00
Clayton, Mark, (WR), Louisville, 1993	4.00	12.00
Clemens, Bob, (B), Georgia, 1955	8.00	20.00
Clemens, Cal, (B), USC, 1936	15.00	40.00
Clemons, Ray, (G), St. Marys, 1947	10.00	30.00
Cloud, Jack, (B), William & Mary, 1950-51	8.00	25.00
Cobb, Reggie, (RB), Tennessee, 1994	4.00	12.00
Cody, Ed, (B), Purdue, 1947-48	10.00	30.00
Coffy, J.R., (RB), Washington, 1965	10.00	25.00
Coffman, Paul, (TE), Kansas State, 1978-85	8.00	25.00
Coleman, Keo, (LB), Mississippi, 1993	3.00	10.00
Collier, Steve, (T), Bethune Cookman, 1987-88	3.00	10.00
Collins, Al, (B), Louisiana State, 1951	8.00	20.00

Player/Position/College/Years with Packers	Price Range	
Collins, Brett, (LB), Washington, 1992-93	3.00	10.00
Collins, Patrick, (RB), Oklahoma, 1988	3.00	10.00
Collins, Shawn, (WR), Northern Arizona, 1993	3.00	10.00
Comp, Irv, (B), St. Benedict, 1943-49	10.00	30.00
Compton, Chuck, (DB), Boise State, 1987	3.00	10.00
Comstock, Rudy, (G), Georgetown, 1931-33	15.00	40.00
Comcannon, Jack, (QB), Boston College, 1974	4.00	12.00
Conway, Dave, (G), Texas, 1971	4.00	12.00
Cone, Fred, (B), Clemson, 1951-57	8.00	25.00
Cook, Jim, (G), Wisconsin, 1921	20.00	75.00
Cook, Kelly, (RB), Oklahoma State, 1987	3.00	10.00
Cook, Ted, (E), Alabama, 1948-50	10.00	25.00
Cooke, Bill, (DE), Massachusetts, 1975	4.00	10.00
Cooney, Mark, (DE), Colorado, 1974	4.00	10.00
Corker, John, (LB), Oklahoma State, 1988	3.00	10.00
Coughlin, Frank, (B), Notre Dame, 1921	20.00	75.00
Coutret, Larry, (B), Notre Dame, 1950, 1953	8.00	25.00
Craig, Larry, (B), South Carolina, 1939-49	15.00	40.00
Crawford, Keith, (CB), Howard Payne, 1995	3.00	10.00
Cremer, Ted, (E), Auburn, 1948	10.00	30.00
Crenshaw, Leon, (DT), Tuskegee, 1968	5.00	12.00
Crimmins, Bernie, (G), Notre Dame, 1945	10.00	25.00
Croft, Milburn, (T), Ripon, 1942-47	10.00	30.00
Cronin, Tom, (B), Marquette, 1922	20.00	55.00
Croston, Dave, (T), Iowa, 1988	3.00	10.00
Crouse, Ray, (RB), Nevada-Las Vegas, 1984	3.00	10.00
Crowley, Jim, (B), Notre Dame (1 of the 4 horseman), 1925	10.00	100.00
Crutcher, Tommy, (LB), TCU, 1964-67, 1971-72	10.00	25.00
Cuff, Ward, (B), Marquette, 1947	10.00	30.00
Cullbreath, Jim, (FB), Oklahoma, 1977-79	3.00	10.00
Culver, Al, (T), Notre Dame, 1932	15.00	40.00
Cumby, George, (LB), Oklahoma, 1980-85	4.00	12.00
Curcio, Mike, (LB), Temple, 1983	3.00	10.00
Currie, Dan, (LB), Michigan State, 1958-64	10.00	25.00
Curry, Bill, (C), Georgia Tech, 1965-66	10.00	25.00
Cvercko, Andy, (G), Northwester, 1960	10.00	25.00

Player/Position/College/Years with Packers	Price Range	
Cyre, Hector, (T), Gonzaga, 1926-28	20.00	25.00

D

Dahms, Tom, (T), San Diego State, 1955	8.00	20.00
Dale, Carroll, (WR), Virginia Tech, 1965-72	10.00	25.00
Danelo, Joe, (K), Washington State, 1975	4.00	10.00
Daniell, Averall, (T), Pittsburgh, 1937	15.00	40.00
Danjean, Ernie, (G), Auburn, 1957	8.00	20.00
Darling, Bernard, (C), Beloit, 1927-31	25.00	30.00
Davenport, Bill, (B), Harden Simmons, 1931	15.00	45.00
Davey, Don, (DE/DT), Wisconsin, 1991-94	4.00	12.00
Davidson, Ben, (T), Washington, 1961	10.00	25.00
Davis, Dave, (WR), Tennessee A&I, 1971-72	4.00	12.00
Davis, Harper, (B), Mississippi State, 1951	8.00	20.00
Davis, Kenneth, (RB), Texas Christian, 1986-88	4.00	10.00
Davis, Paul, (G), Marquette, 1922	20.00	60.00
Davis, Ralph, (G), Wisconsin, 1947-48	10.00	30.00
Davis, Wille, (DE), Grambling, (HOF), 1960-69	15.00	35.00
Dawson, Dale, (K), Eastern Kentucky, 1988	3.00	10.00
Dawson, Gib, (B), Texas, 1953	8.00	20.00
Dean, Walter, (FB), Grambling, 1991	3.00	10.00
Deeks, Don, (T), Texas, 1938	10.00	30.00
Dees, Bob, (T), Southwest Missouri State, 1952	8.00	20.00
Degrate, Tony, (DE), Texas, 1985	3.00	10.00
Del Gazio, Jim, (QB), Tampa, 1973	4.00	10.00
Del Greco, Al, (K), Auburn, 1984-87	4.00	10.00
DeLisle, Jim, (DT), Wisconsin, 1971	3.00	10.00
De Luca, Tony, (NT), Rhode Island, 1984	3.00	10.00
DeMoe, Bill, (E), Beloit, 1921	20.00	75.00
Dennard, Preston, (WR), New Mexico, 1985	3.00	10.00
Dent, Burnell, (LB), Tulane, 1986-92	4.00	12.00
Dechaine, Dick, (E), no college, 1955-57	8.00	20.00
Detmer, Ty, (QB), Brigham Young, 1992-95	5.00	20.00
Dickey, Lynn, (QB), Kansas State, 1976-77, 1979-85	8.00	15.00
Didier, Clint, (TE), Portland State, 1988-89	3.00	10.00
Dillon, Bobby, (B), Texas, 1952-59	10.00	25.00

Player/Position/College/Years with Packers		Price Range
Dilweg, Anthony, (QB), Duke, 1989-90	3.00	10.00
Dilweg, Lavvie, (E), Marquette, 1927-34	35.00	75.00
Dimler, Rich, (T), USC, 1980	3.00	10.00
DiPierro, Ray, (G), Ohio State, 1950-51	8.00	20.00
Disend, Leo, (T), Albright, 1940	10.00	30.00
Dittrich, John, (G), Wisconsin, 1959	8.00	20.00
Don Carlos, John, (C), Drake, 1931	15.00	45.00
D'Onofrio, Mark, (LB), Penn State, 1992	3.00	10.00
Donhoe, Mike, (TE), San Francisco, 1973-74	4.00	12.00
Dorsett, Mathew, (CB), Southern, 1995	3.00	10.00
Dorsey, Dean, (K), Toronto, 1988	3.00	10.00
Dorsey, John, (LB), Connecticut, 1984-88	4.00	10.00
Dotson, Earl, (T), Texas A&I, 1993-	10.00	20.00
Douglas, George, (C), Marquette, 1921	25.00	75.00
Douglass, Bobby, (QB), Kansas, 1978	4.00	12.00
Douglass, Mike, (LB), San Diego State, 1978-85	5.00	15.00
Dowden, Steve, (T), Baylor, 1952	8.00	20.00
Dowler, Boyd, (E), Colorado, 1959-69	10.00	25.00
Dowling, Brian, (QB), Yale, 1977	4.00	10.00
Drechsler, Dave, (G), North Carolina, 1983-84	3.00	10.00
Dreyer, Wally, (B), Wisconsin, 1950-51	8.00	20.00
Drost, Jeff, (DT), Iowa, 1987	3.00	10.00
Drulis, Chuck, (G), Temple, 1950	8.00	20.00
Duckett, Forey, (CB), Nevada-Reno, 1994	3.00	10.00
Duford, Wilfred, (B), Marquette, 1924	20.00	45.00
Duhart, Paul, (B), Florida, 1944	10.00	35.00
Dukes, Jamie, (C), Florida State, 1994	3.00	10.00
Dunaway, Dave, (E), Duke, 1968	4.00	12.00
Duncan, Ken, (P/WR), Tulsa, 1971	4.00	12.00
Dunn, Red, (B), Marquette, 1927-31	20.00	60.00
Dunningan, Walt, (E), Minnesota, 1922	25.00	65.00

E

Earhart, Ralph, (B), Texas Tech, 1948-49	10.00	30.00
Earp, Jug, (C), Monmout, 1922-32	25.00	65.00
Eason, Roger, (T), Oklahoma, 1949	10.00	30.00

Player/Position/College/Years with Packers		Price Range
Ecker, Ed, (T), John Carroll, 1950-51	8.00	25.00
Edwards, Earl, (DT), Wichita State, 1979	4.00	12.00
Ellersons, Gary, (FB),Wisconsin, 1985-86	3.00	10.00
Elliott, Burton, (B), Marquette, 1921	25.00	75.00
Elliott, Carleton, (E), Virginia, 1951-54	8.00	25.00
Elliott, Tony, (DB), Central Michigan, 1987-88	3.00	10.00
Ellis, Gerry, (FB), Missouri, 1980-86	5.00	12.00
Ellis, Ken, (DB), Southern, 1970-75	4.00	12.00
Enderle, Dick, (G), Minnesota, 1976	4.00	10.00
Engebretsen, Paul, (G), Northwestern, 1934-41	20.00	45.00
Engelmann, Wuert, (B), South Dakota State, 1930-33	20.00	45.00
Enright, Rex, (B), Notre Dame, 1926-27	25.00	60.00
Epps, Phillip, (WR), Texas Christian, 1982-88	5.00	15.00
Erickson, Harry, (B), Washington & Jefferson, 1923	25.00	65.00
Estep, Mike, (G), Bowling Green, 1987	3.00	10.00
Estes, Roy, (B), Georgia, 1928	20.00	55.00
Ethridge, Joe, (T), Southern Methodist, 1949	10.00	30.00
Evans, Dick, (E), Iowa, 1940, 1943	10.00	30.00
Evans, Doug, (CB), Louisiana Tech, 1993-	10.00	25.00
Evans, John, (B), California, 1929	20.00	60.00
Evans, Lon, (G), Texas Christian, 1933-37	15.00	50.00

F

Falkenstein, Tony, (B), St. Mary's, 1943	10.00	30.00
Fanucci, Mike, (DE), Arizona State, 1974	4.00	10.00
Faverty, Hal, (C), Wisconsin, 1952	8.00	25.00
Favre, Brett, (QB), Southern Mississippi, 1992-	25.00	75.00
Faye, Allen, (E), Marquette, 1922	25.00	55.00
Feasel, Greg, (T), Abilene Christian, 1986	3.00	10.00
Feathers, Beattie, (B), Tennessee, 1940	10.00	35.00
Felker, Art, (E), Marquette, 1951	8.00	25.00
Ferguson, Howie, (B), no college, 1953-58	10.00	25.00
Ferragamo, Vince, (QB), Nebraska, 1985-86	5.00	12.00
Ferry, Lou, (T), Villanova, 1949	10.00	30.00
Fields, Angelo, (T), Michigan State, 1982	3.00	10.00
Finely, Jim, (G), Michigan State, 1942	10.00	30.00

Finnin, Tom, (T), Detroit, 1957 ....8.00   25.00
Fitzgerald, Kevin, (TE), Wisconsin-Eau Claire, 1987 ....3.00   10.00
Fitzgibbons, Paul, (B), Crieghton, 1930-32 ....20.00   55.00
Flaherty, Dick, (E), Marquette, 1926-27 ....25.00   50.00
Flanigan, Jim, (LB), Pittsburgh, 1967-70 ....8.00   25.00
Fleming, Marv, (E), Utah, 1963-69 ....10.00   25.00
Flowers, Bob, (C), Texas Tech, 1942-48 ....10.00   30.00
Floyd, Bobby Jack, (B), Texas Christian, 1952, 1954 ....8.00   25.00
Flynn, Tom, (S), Pittsburgh, 1984-86 ....4.00   10.00
Folkins, Lee, (E), Washington, 1961 ....10.00   25.00
Fontenot, Herman, (RB), Louisiana State, 1989-90 ....4.00   10.00
Ford, Len, (E), Michigan, (HOF), 1958 ....15.00   40.00
Forester, Bill, (LB), Southern Methodist, 1953-63 ....10.00   25.00
Forte, Aldo, (G), Montana, 1947 ....15.00   35.00
Forte, Bob, (B), Arkansas, 1946-53 ....15.00   40.00
Francis, Joe, (B), Oregon State, 1958-60 ....8.00   25.00
Frankowski, Bob, (G), Washington, 1945 ....15.00   35.00
Franta, Herb, (T), St. Thomas, 1930 ....25.00   55.00
Franz, Nolan, (WR), Tulane, 1986 ....3.00   10.00
Freeman, Antonio, (WR), Virginia Tech, 1995- 10.00   25.00
Freeman, Bob, (B), Auburn, 1959 ....8.00   25.00
Fries, Sherwood, (G), Colorado State, 1943 ....15.00   35.00
Fritsch, Ted, (B), Stevens Point Teachers', 1942-50 ....15.00   40.00
Frutig, Ed, (E), Michigan, 1941-45 ....15.00   40.00
Fuller, Joe, (CB), Northern Iowa, 1991 ....3.00   10.00
Fullwood, Brent, (RB), Auburn, 1987-90 ....4.00   12.00
Fusina, Chuck, (QB), Penn State, 1986 ....3.00   10.00

G

Gabbard, Steve, (T), Florida State, 1991 ....3.00   10.00
Galbreath, Harry, (G), Tennessee, 1993-95 ....3.00   10.00
Gantenbein, Milt, (E), Wisconsin, 1931-40 ....20.00   55.00
Garcia, Eddie, (K), Southern Methodist, 1983-84 ....3.00   10.00
Gardella, Augustus, (B), Holy Cross, 1922 ....25.00   65.00
Gardner, Milt, (G), Wisconsin, 1922-26 ....25.00   65.00
Garrett, Bob, (B), Stanford, 1954 ....8.00   25.00

Player/Position/College/Years with Packers	Price Range	
Garrett, Len, (TE), N.M. Highlands, 1971-72	4.00	12.00
Gassert, Ron, (T), Virginia, 1962	10.00	25.00
Gatewood, Lester, (C), Baylor, 1946-47	15.00	35.00
Gavin, Fritz, (E), Marquette, 1921, 1923	25.00	70.00
Gaydos, Kent, (WR), Florida State, 1975	4.00	10.00
Getty, Charlie, (T), Penn State, 1983	3.00	10.00
Gibson, Paul, (WR), Florida State, 1975	4.00	12.00
Gillette, Jim, (B), Virginia, 1947	15.00	45.00
Gillingham, Gale, (G), Minnesota, 1966-74, 1976	10.00	25.00
Gillus, Willie, (QB), Norfolk State, 1987	3.00	10.00
Girard, Jug, (B), Wisconsin, 1948-51	15.00	40.00
Glass, Leland, (WR), Oregon, 1972-73	4.00	12.00
Glick, Eddie, (B), Marquette, 1921-22	25.00	75.00
Gofourth, Derrel, (C), Oklahoma State, 1977-82	4.00	12.00
Goldenberg, Charles, (G), Wisconsin, 1933-45	25.00	75.00
Goodman, Les, (RB), Yankton, 1973-74	4.00	12.00
Goodnight, Clyde, (E), Tulsa, 1945-49	15.00	40.00
Gordon, Dick, (WR), Michigan State, 1973	4.00	12.00
Gordon, Lou, (T), Illinois, 1936-37	20.00	55.00
Gorgal, Ken, (B), Purdue, 1956	8.00	25.00
Grabowski, Jim, (B), Illinois, 1966-70	10.00	25.00
Grant, David, (DE), West Virginia, 1993	3.00	10.00
Gray, Cecil, (T), North Carolina, 1992	3.00	10.00
Gray, Jack, (E), no college, 1923	25.00	65.00
Gray, Johnnie, (DB), Cal St.-Fullerton, 1975-84	5.00	15.00
Green, Jessie, (WR), Tulsa, 1976	4.00	10.00
Greene, Tiger, (S), Western Carolina, 1986-90	3.00	10.00
Greeney, Norm, (G), Notre Dame, 1933	20.00	50.00
Greenfield, Tom, (C), Iowa, 1928	25.00	65.00
Greenwood, David, (DB), Wisconsin, 1986	3.00	10.00
Gregg, Forrest, (T), Southern Methodist, (HOF), 1956, 1958-70	12.00	30.00
Gremminger, Hank, (B), Baylor, 1956-65	10.00	25.00
Griffen, Harold, (C), Iowa, 1928	25.00	65.00
Grimes, Billy, (B), Oklahoma A&M, 1950-52	8.00	25.00
Grimm, Dan, (G), Colorado, 1963-65	10.00	25.00
Gros, Earl, (B), Louisiana State, 1962-63	10.00	25.00

Player/Position/College/Years with Packers	_Price Range_	
Grove, Roger, (B), Michigan State, 1931-35	20.00	50.00
Gruber, Bob, (T), Pittsburgh, 1987	3.00	10.00
Gudauskas, Pete, (G), Murray State, 1942, 1945	10.00	30.00
Gueno, Jim, (LB), Tulane, 1976-80	3.00	10.00
Gudie, Walter, (G), Wisconsin, 1943-44	10.00	30.00

H

Hackbart, Dale, (B), Wisconsin, 1960	10.00	25.00
Hackett, Joey, (TE), Elon, 1987-88	3.00	10.00
Haddix, Michael, (FB), Mississippi, 1989-90	3.00	10.00
Hadl, John, (QB), Kansas, 1974-75	5.00	15.00
Haley, Darryl, (T), Utah, 1988	3.00	10.00
Hall, Charles, (DB), Pittsburgh, 1971-76	4.00	10.00
Hall, Mark, (DE), Southwestern La, 1989-90	3.00	10.00
Hallstrom, Ron, (G), Iowa, 1982-92	4.00	10.00
Hamilton, Ruffin, (LB), Tulane, 1994	3.00	10.00
Hampton, Dave, (RB), Wyoming, 1969-71	3.00	10.00
Hanner, Dave, (DT), Arkansas, 1952-64	10.00	30.00
Hanny, Frank, (T), Indiana, 1930	20.00	50.00
Hansen, Don, (LB), Illinois, 1976-77	4.00	10.00
Hanson, Roy, (B), Marquette, 1923	25.00	60.00
Harden, Derrick, (WR), Eastern New Mexico, 1987	3.00	10.00
Harden, Leon (DS), Texas-El Paso, 1970	4.00	10.00
Harding, Roger, (C), California, 1949	10.00	30.00
Hardy, Kevin, (DT), Notre Dame, 1970	4.00	10.00
Hargrove, James, (RB), Wake Forest, 1987	3.00	10.00
Harrell, Willard, (RB), Pacific, 1975-77	4.00	12.00
Harris, Bernardo, (LB), North Carolina, 1995-	10.00	25.00
Harris, Corey, (WR/CB/KR), Vanderbilt, 1992-94	4.00	10.00
Harris, Jackie, (TE), Northeast La, 1990-93	4.00	10.00
Harris, Leotis, (G), Arkansas, 1978-83	3.00	10.00
Harris, Tim, (LB), Memphis State, 1986-90	4.00	12.00
Harris, William, (TE), Bishop College, 1990	3.00	10.00
Harris, W.W. "Jack," (B), Wisconsin, 1925-26	25.00	60.00
Harrison, Anthony, (DB), Georgia Tech, 1987	3.00	10.00
Harrison, Reggie, (RB), Cincinnati, 1978	3.00	10.00

Player/Position/College/Years with Packers   *Price Range*

Hart, Doug, (DB), Texas-Arlington, 1964-71 ....10.00   25.00

Hartnett, Perry, (G), Colorado, 1987 ....3.00   10.00

Hartwig, Keith, (WR), Arizona, 1977 ....4.00   10.00

Harvey, Maurice, (S), Ball State, 1981-83 ....3.00   10.00

Hathock, Dave, (B), Memphis State, 1966 ....10.00   25.00

Hauck, Tim, (S), Montana, 1991-94 ....3.00   10.00

Havig, Dennis, (G), Colorado, 1977 ....4.00   10.00

Haycraft, Ken, (E), Wisconsin, 1964-66 ....10.00   25.00

Hayes, Gary, (DB), Fresno State, 1984-86 ....3.00   10.00

Hayes, Norb, (E), Marquette, 1923 ....25.00   60.00

Hayhoe, Bill, (T), USC, 1969-74 ....4.00   12.00

Hays, Dave, (E), Notre Dame, 1921-22 ....25.00   75.00

Hays, George, (E), St. Bonaventure, 1953 ....8.00   25.00

Hearden, Les, (B), St. Ambrose, 1924 ....25.00   60.00

Hearden, Tom, (B), Notre Dame, 1927-28 ....25.00   50.00

Heath, Stan, (B), Nevada, 1949 ....10.00   30.00

Hefner, Larry, (LB), Clemson, 1972-75 ....4.00   10.00

Held, Paul, (QB), San Diego State, 1955 ....8.00   25.00

Helluin, Jerry, (T), Tulane, 1954-57 ....8.00   25.00

Henderson, William, (FB), North Carolina, 1995- 10.00   25.00

Hendarian, Warren, (B), Pittsburgh, 1924 ....25.00   60.00

Hendricks, Ted, (LB), Miami, (HOF), 1974 ....10.00   30.00

Henry, Urban, (T), Georgia Tech, 1963 ....8.00   20.00

Hentrich, Craig, (P), Notre Dame, 1994- 10.00   25.00

Herber, Arnie, (B), Regis, (HOF), 1930-41 ....25.00   65.00

Hickman, Larry, (B), Baylor, 1960 ....10.00   25.00

Highsmith, Don, (RB), Michigan State, 1973 ....4.00   10.00

Hill, Don, (B), Stanford, 1929 ....20.00   55.00

Hill, Jim, (DB), Texas A&M, 1972-74 ....4.00   10.00

Hill, Nate, (DE), Auburn, 1988 ....3.00   10.00

Hilton, John, (TE), Richmond, 1970 ....4.00   10.00

Himes, Dick, (T), Ohio State, 1968-77 ....5.00   12.00

Hinkle, Clarke, (B), Bucknell, (HOF), 1932-41 ....25.00   60.00

Hinte, Tex, (E), Pittsburgh, 1941 ....10.00   30.00

Hobbins, Jim, (G), Minnesota, 1987 ....3.00   10.00

Hoffman, Gary, (T), Santa Clara, 1984 ....3.00   10.00

Player/Position/College/Years with Packers	*Price Range*	
Holland, Darius, (DT), Colorado, 1995-	10.00	25.00
Holland, Johnny, (LB), Texas A&M, 1987-93	3.00	10.00
Holler, Ed, (LB), South Carolina, 1963	8.00	20.00
Homes, Jerry, (CB), West Virginia, 1990-91	3.00	10.00
Hood, Estus, (DB), Illinois State, 1978-84	4.00	12.00
Hope, Charles, (G), Central (Ohio) State, 1994	3.00	10.00
Horn, Don, (QB), San Diego State, 1967-70	8.00	20.00
Hornung, Paul, (B), Notre Dame, (HOF), 1957-62, 1964-66	15.00	35.00
Houston, Bobby, (LB), North Carolina State, 1990	3.00	10.00
Howard, Desmond, (WR), Michigan, 1996	15.00	35.00
Howard, Lynn, (B), Indiana, 1921-22	25.00	75.00
Howell, John, (B), Nebraska, 1938	20.00	45.00
Howton, Bill, (E), Rice, 1952-58	8.00	25.00
Hubbard, Cal, (T), Centenary Geneva, 1929-35	15.00	25.00
Huckleby, Harlan, (RB), Michigan, 1980-85	4.00	12.00
Hudson, Bob, (RB), Northeastern (Okla.) State, 1972	4.00	12.00
Hudson, Craig, (TE), Wisconsin, 1990	3.00	10.00
Huffman, Tim, (T), Notre Dame, 1981-85	3.00	10.00
Hull, Tom, (LB), Penn State, 1975	4.00	10.00
Humphrey, Donnie, (DE), Auburn, 1984-86	3.00	10.00
Hunt, Ervin, (DB), Fresno State, 1970	4.00	10.00
Hunt, Kevin, (T), Doane (Neb.), 1972	4.00	10.00
Hunt, Michael, (LB), Minnesota, 1978-80	4.00	10.00
Hunt, Sam, (LB), Stephan F. Austin, 1980	3.00	10.00
Hunter, Art, (C), Notre Dame, 1954	8.00	25.00
Hunter, Scott, (QB), Alabama, 1971-73	4.00	12.00
Hunter, Tony, (RB), Minnesota, 1987	3.00	10.00
Hutchins, Paul, (T), Western Michigan, 1993-94	3.00	10.00
Hutson, Don, (E), Alabama, (HOF), 1935-45	25.00	75.00
Hyland, Bob, (C), Boston College, 1967-69, 1976	8.00	25.00

I

Ilkin, Tunch, (T), Indiana State, 1993	3.00	10.00
Iman, Ken, (C), Southeast Missouri State, 1960-63	10.00	25.00
Ingalls, Bob, (C), Michigan, 1942	10.00	30.00
Ingram, Darryl, (TE), California, 1992-93	3.00	10.00

Player/Position/College/Years with Packers	*Price Range*	
Ingram, Mark, (WR), Michigan State, 1995	3.00	10.00
Isbell, Cecil, (B), Purdue, 1938-42	15.00	45.00
Ivery, Eddie Lee, (RB), Georgia Tech, 1979-86	8.00	20.00

J

Jacke, Chris, (K), Texas-El Paso, 1989-96	10.00	25.00
Jackson, Johnnie, (S), Houston, 1992	3.00	10.00
Jackson, Keith, (TE), Oklahoma, 1996	10.00	25.00
Jackson, Mel (G), USC, 1976-80	4.00	10.00
Jacobs, Allen, (B), Utah, 1965	10.00	25.00
Jacobs, Jack, (B), Oklahoma, 1947-49	10.00	30.00
Jacunski, Harry, (E), Fordham, 1939-44	12.00	40.00
Jakes, Van, (CB), Kent State, 1989	3.00	10.00
James, Claudis, (FL), Jackson State, 1967-69	8.00	25.00
Jankowski, Eddie, (B), Wisconsin, 1937-41	12.00	30.00
Jansante, Val, (E), Duquesne, 1951	8.00	25.00
Jay, Craig, (TE), Mount Senario, 1987	3.00	10.00
Jean, Walter, (G), Missouri, 1925-26	25.00	60.00
Jefferson, John, (WR), Arizona State, 1981-84	3.00	10.00
Jenison, Ray, (T), South Dakota State, 1987-88	20.00	50.00
Jenke, Noel, (LB), Minnesota, 1973-74	4.00	10.00
Jennings, Jim, (E), Missouri, 1955	8.00	25.00
Jensen, Greg, (G), no college, 1987	3.00	10.00
Jensen, Jim, (RB), Iowa, 1981-82	3.00	10.00
Jervey, Travis, (RB), The Citadel, 1995-	10.00	25.00
Jeter, Bob, (DB), Iowa, 1963-70	10.00	25.00
Johnson, Bill, (E), Minnesota, 1941	3.00	10.00
Johnson, Charles, (DT), Maryland, 1979-80, 1983	3.00	10.00
Johnson, Danny, (LB), Tennessee State, 1978	3.00	10.00
Johnson, Ezra, (DE), Morris Brown, 1977-87	4.00	12.00
Johnson, Glen, (T), Arizona State, 1949	10.00	30.00
Johnson, Howard, (G), Georgia, 1940-41	10.00	30.00
Johnson, Joe, (B), Boston College, 1954-58	8.00	25.00
Johnson, Kenneth, (DB), Mississippi State, 1987	3.00	10.00
Johnson, KeShon, (CB), Arizona, 1994	3.00	10.00
Johnson, LeShon, (RB), Northern Illinois, 1994-95	4.00	12.00

Johnson, Marv, (B), San Jose State, 1952-53	8.00	25.00
Johnson, Randy, (QB), Texas A&I, 1976	4.00	10.00
Johnson, Reggie, (TE), Florida State, 1994	3.00	10.00
Johnson, Sammy Lee, (B), North Carolina, 1979	3.00	10.00
Johnson, Tom, (T), Michigan, 1952	10.00	25.00
Johnston, Chester, (B), Marquette, 1934-39	20.00	50.00
Johnstone, Art, (B), Lawrence, 1931	20.00	50.00
Jolly, Mike, (S), Michigan, 1980-83	3.00	10.00
Jones, Bob, (G), Indiana, 1934	20.00	50.00
Jones, Bruce, (G), Alabama, 1927-28	25.00	60.00
Jones, Daryll, (DB), Georgia, 1984-85	3.00	10.00
Jones, Ron, (TE), Texas-El Paso, 1969	4.00	12.00
Jones, Scott, (T), Washington, 1991	3.00	10.00
Jones, Sean, (DE), Northeastern, 1994-96	10.00	25.00
Jones, Terry, (DL), Alabama, 1978-84	3.00	10.00
Jones, Tom, (G), Bucknell, 1938	20.00	50.00
Jordan, Charles, (WR), Long Beach City, 1994-95	3.00	10.00
Jordan, Henry, (DT), Virginia, (HOF), 1959-69	70.00	150.00
Jordan, Kenneth, (LB), Tuskegee, 1987	3.00	10.00
Jorgenson, Carl, (T), St. Marys, 1934	20.00	25.00
Jurkovic, John, (NT), Eastern Illinois, 1991-95	3.00	10.00

K

Kahler, Bob, (B), Nebraska, 1941-44	15.00	35.00
Kahler, Royal, (T), Nebraska, 1942	15.00	35.00
Kalosh, Mike, (E), La Crosse State Teachers, 1948	15.00	35.00
Katalininas, Leo, (T), Catholic University, 1938	20.00	45.00
Kauahi, Kani, (C), Hawaii, 1988	3.00	10.00
Keane, Jim, (E), Iowa, 1952	8.00	25.00
Keefe, Emmett, (T), Notre Dame, 1921	25.00	75.00
Kekeris, Jim, (T), Texas Tech, 1948	15.00	35.00
Kemp, Perry, (WR), California (Pa.) University, 1988-91	3.00	10.00
Kenyon, Crowell, (G), Ripon, 1923	25.00	65.00
Kercher, Bob, (E), Georgetown, 1944	15.00	35.00
Kern, Bill, (T), Pittsburgh, 1929-30	25.00	65.00
Kueper, Ken, (B), Georgia, 1945-47	15.00	35.00

Player/Position/College/Years with Packers   Price Range

Kiel, Blair, (QB), Notre Dame, 1988-91...3.00   10.00

Kiesling, Walt, (G), St. Thomas, (HOF), 1935-36................................50.00   125.00

Kilbourn, Warren, (T), Michigan, 1939..20.00   50.00

Kimball, Bob, (WR), Oklahoma, 1979-80..3.00   10.00

Kimmel, J.D., (T), Houston, 1958 ....8.00   25.00

Kinard, Bill, (B), Mississippi, 1957-58...10.00   30.00

King, David, (DB), Auburn, 1987 ....3.00   10.00

King, Don, (T), Kentucky, 1956 ....8.00   25.00

King, Don, (DB), Southern Methodist, 1987...3.00   10.00

Kirby, John, (B), USC, 1949..10.00   30.00

Kitson, Syd, (G), Wake Forest, 1980-81, 1983-84 ....3.00   10.00

Klaus, Fee, (C), no college, 1921..25.00   75.00

Kiebhan, Adolph, (B), Milwaukee Teachers, 1921 ....25.00   75.00

Koart, Matt, (LB), USC, 1986 ....3.00   10.00

Koch, Greg, (T), Arkansas, 1977-85..3.00   10.00

Koncar, Mark, (T), Colorado, 1976-81 ....3.00   10.00

Koonce, Georga, (LB), East Carolina, 1992-..10.00   25.00

Kopay, Dave, (B), Washington, 1972...4.00   10.00

Knafelc, Gary, (E), Colorado, 1954-62..10.00   25.00

Knapp, Lindsay, (G), Notre Dame, 1995-96...8.00   15.00

Knutson, Gene, (E), Michigan, 1954-56...8.00   25.00

Knutson, Steve, (T), USC, 1976-77 ....4.00   12.00

Konopasek, Ed, (T), Ball State, 1987 ....3.00   10.00

Kostelnik, Ron, (T), Cincinnati, 1961-68 ....15.00   45.00

Kotal, Eddie, (B), Lawerence, 1925-29 ....25.00   65.00

Kovatch, John, (E), Notre Dame, 1947..10.00   30.00

Kowalkowski, Bob, (G), Virginia, 1977...4.00   10.00

Kramer, Jerry, (G), Idaho, 1958-68 ....10.00   25.00

Kramer, Ron, (TE), Michigan, 1957, 1959-64.......................................10.00   25.00

Kranz, Ken, (B), Milwaukee Teachers, 1949...10.00   30.00

Krause, Larry, (RB), St. Norbert, 1970-74 ....4.00   10.00

Kresky, Joe, (G), Wisconsin, 1930 ....20.00   55.00

Kroll, Bob, (DB), Northern Michigan, 1972-73 ....4.00   10.00

Kuberski, Bob, (NT), Navy, 1995...10.00   25.00

Kuechenberg, Rudy, (LB), Indiana, 1970...4.00   10.00

Kuick, Stan, (B), Beloit, 1926..25.00   60.00

Player/Position/College/Years with Packers	*Price Range*	
Kurth, Joe, (T), Notre Dame, 1933-34	20.00	50.00
Kuusisto, Bill, (G), Minnesota, 1941-46	10.00	30.00

L

Laabs, Kermit, (B), Beloit, 1925	25.00	65.00
Labbe, Rico, (S), Boston College, 1990	3.00	10.00
LaBounty, Matt, (DE), Oregon, 1995	3.00	10.00
Ladrow, Wally, (B), no college, 1921	25.00	75.00
Lally, Bob, (LB), Cornell, 1976	4.00	10.00
Lambeau, Earl "Curly," (B), Notre Dame, (HOF), 1921-30	200.00	500.00
Lammons, Pete, (TE), Texas, 1972	4.00	10.00
Lande, Cliff, (E), Carroll, 1921	25.00	75.00
Landers, Walt, (RB), Clark College, 1978-79	4.00	10.00
Lane, MacArthur, (RB), Utah State, 1972-74	5.00	15.00
Lankas, Jim, (B), St. Mary's, 1943	10.00	30.00
Larson, Bill, (TE), Colorado State, 1980	3.00	10.00
Larson, Fred, (C), Notre Dame, 1925	25.00	60.00
Larson, Kurt, (LB), Michigan State, 1991	3.00	10.00
Laslavic, Jim, (LB), Penn State, 1982	3.00	10.00
Lathrop, Kit, (DT), Arizona State, 1979-80	3.00	10.00
Lauer, John, (B), Detroit, 1922	25.00	65.00
Lauer, Larry, (C), Alabama, 1956-57	8.00	25.00
Laughlin, Jim, (LB), Ohio State, 1983	3.00	10.00
Lawrence, Jim, (B), Texas Christian, 1939	20.00	50.00
Laws, Joe, (B), Iowa, 1934-35	20.00	60.00
Leaper, Wesley, (E), Wisconsin, 1921, 1923	25.00	75.00
Lee, Bill, (T), Alabama, 1937-42, 1946	20.00	55.00
Lee, Mark, (CB), Washington, 1980-90	4.00	12.00
Leigh, Charlie, (RB), no college, 1974	4.00	10.00
Leiker, Tony, (DE), Stanford, 1987	3.00	10.00
Leopold, Bobby, (LB), Notre Dame, 1986	3.00	10.00
Lester, Darrell, (C), Texas Christian, 1937-38	10.00	30.00
Letlow, Russ, (G), San Francisco, 1936-42, 1946	12.00	35.00
Levens, Dorsey, (RB), Georgia Tech, 1994-	10.00	25.00
Lewellen, Verne, (B), Nebraska, 1924-32	25.00	60.00
Lewis, Cliff, (LB), Southern Mississippi, 1981-84	3.00	10.00

Player/Position/College/Years with Packers	*Price Range*	
Lewis, Gary, (TE), Texas-Arlington, 1981-84	3.00	10.00
Lewis, Mark, (TE), Texas A&M, 1985-87	3.00	10.00
Lewis, Mike, (NT), Arkansas A&M, 1980	3.00	10.00
Lewis, Ron, (WR), Florida State, 1992-94	3.00	10.00
Lewis, Tim, (CB), Pittsburgh, 1983-86	3.00	10.00
Lidberg, Carl, (B), Minnesota, 1926-30	25.00	65.00
Lipscomb, Paul, (T), Tennessee, 1945-49	15.00	35.00
Liscio, Tony, (T), Tulsa, 1963	8.00	20.00
Livingston, Dale, (K), Western Michigan, 1970	4.00	12.00
Lofton, James, (WR), Stanford, 1978-86	8.00	25.00
Logan, David, (NT), Pittsburgh, 1987	3.00	10.00
Logan, Dick, (T), Ohio State, 1952-53	8.00	25.00
Lollar, George, (B), Howard, 1928	25.00	50.00
Long, Bob, (E), Wichita, 1964-67	10.00	25.00
Loomis, Ace, (B), La Crosse State Teachers, 1951-53	8.00	25.00
Losch, John, (B), Miami, 1956	8.00	25.00
Lucky, Bill, (T), Arizona, 1968-74	5.00	15.00
Ludtke, Norm, (G), Carroll, 1924	25.00	55.00
Lueck, Bill, (G), Arizona, 1968-74	5.00	15.00
Luhn, Nolan, (E), Tulsa, 1945-49	10.00	30.00
Luke, Steve, (DB), Ohio State, 1975-80	4.00	10.00
Lusteg, Booth, (K), Connecticut, 1969-70	4.00	10.00
Lyle, Dewey, (E), Minnesota, 1922-23	25.00	65.00
Lyman, Del, (T), UCLA, 1941	10.00	30.00

M

Mass, Bill, (NT), Pittsburgh, 1993	3.00	10.00
MacAuliffe, John, (B), Beloit, 1926	25.00	75.00
Mack, "Red," (E), Notre Dame, 1966	10.00	25.00
MacLeod, Tom, (LB), Minnesota, 1973	4.00	10.00
Maddox, George, (T), Kansas State, 1935	15.00	35.00
Majkowski, Don, (QB), Virginia, 1987-92	5.00	15.00
Maloncon, Rydell, (LB), Louisiana State, 1987	3.00	10.00
Malone, Grover, (B), Notre Dame, 1921	25.00	75.00
Mandarich, Tony, (T), Michigan State, 1989-91	4.00	10.00
Mandeville, Chris, (DB), California-Davis, 1987-88	3.00	10.00

Player/Position/College/Years with Packers	Price Range	
Manley, Leon, (G), Oklahoma, 1950-51	8.00	25.00
Mann, Bob, (E), Michigan, 1950-54	8.00	24.00
Mann, Erroll, (K), North Dakota, 1968, 1976	4.00	12.00
Mansfield, Von, (DB), Wisconsin, 1987	3.00	10.00
Marcol, Chester, (K), Hillsdale, 1972-80	5.00	15.00
Marks, Larry, (B), Indiana, 1928	25.00	65.00
Marshall, Rich, (T), Stephen F. Austin, 1965	8.00	20.00
Martell, Herman, (E), no college, 1921	25.00	75.00
Martin, Charles, (DE), Livingston, 1984-87	3.00	10.00
Martinkovic, John, (E), Xavier, 1951-56	8.00	25.00
Mason, Dave, (DB), Nebraska, 1974	4.00	10.00
Mason, Joel, (E), Western Michigan, 1941-45	10.00	45.00
Mason, Larry, (RB), Troy State, 1988	3.00	10.00
Massey, Carlton, (E), Texas, 1957-58	8.00	25.00
Masters, Norm, (T), Michigan State, 1957-64	10.00	25.00
Mataele, Stan, (LB), Arizona, 1987	3.00	10.00
Mathys, Charley, (B), Indiana, 1922-26	25.00	65.00
Matson, Pat, (G), Oregon, 1974	4.00	10.00
Matthews, Al, (DB), Texas A&I, 1970-75	4.00	10.00
Matthews, Aubrey, (WR), Delta State, 1988-89	3.00	10.00
Mattos, Harry, (B), St. Marys, 1936	20.00	45.00
Matuszak, Marv, (LB), Tulsa, 1958	8.00	25.00
Mayer, Frank, (G), Notre Dame, 1927	25.00	55.00
McBride, Ron, (RB), Missouri, 1973	4.00	10.00
McCaffrey, Bob, (C), USC, 1975	4.00	10.00
McCarren, Larry, (C), Illinois, 1973-84	5.00	15.00
McCloughan, Dave, (CB), Colorado, 1992	3.00	10.00
McConkey, Phil, (WR), Navy, 1986	3.00	10.00
McCoy, Mike C., (DB), Colorado, 1976-83	4.00	12.00
McCoy, Mike P., (DT), Notre Dame, 1970-76	4.00	12.00
McCrary, Hurdis, (B), Georgia, 1929-33	25.00	65.00
McDougal, Bob, (B), Miami, 1947	15.00	45.00
McDowell, John, (G), St. John's, 1964	8.00	20.00
McGarry, John, (G), St. Joseph's, 1987	3.00	10.00
McGaw, Walter, (G), Beloit, 1926	25.00	55.00
McGeary, Clink, (T), North Dakota, 1950	8.00	25.00

Player/Position/College/Years with Packers	Price Range	
McGee, Buford, (FB), Mississippi, 1992	3.00	10.00
McGee, Max, (E), Tulane, 1954, 1957-67	10.00	25.00
McGeorge, Rich, (TE), Elon, 1970-78	4.00	12.00
McGill, Lenny, (CB), Arizona State, 1994-95	4.00	10.00
McGrew, Sylvester, (DE), Tulane, 1987	3.00	10.00
McGuder, Michael, (CB), Kent State, 1989	3.00	10.00
McHan, Lamar, (B), Arkansas, 1959-60	10.00	25.00
McIlhenny, Don, (B), Southern Methodist, 1957-69	8.00	25.00
McIntyre, Guy, (G), Georgia, 1994	3.00	10.00
McJulien, Paul, (P), Jackson State, 1991-92	3.00	10.00
McKay, Roy, (B), Texas, 1944-47	10.00	30.00
McLaughlin, Joe, (LB), Massachusetts, 1979	3.00	10.00
McLaughlin, Lee, (G), Virginia, 1941	10.00	30.00
McLean, Orlo, (B), no college, 1921	25.00	75.00
McLeod, Mike, (DB), Montana State, 1984-85	3.00	10.00
McMahon, Jim, (QB), Brigham Young, 1995-96	10.00	25.00
McMath, Herb (OL), Morningside, 1977	4.00	10.00
McMichael, Steve, (DT), Texas, 1994	3.00	10.00
McMillan, Ernie, (T), Illinois, 1975	4.00	10.00
McNabb, Dexter, (FB), Florida, 1992-93	3.00	10.00
McNally (Blood), Johnny, (B), St. John's, (HOF), 1928-36	25.00	100.00
McPartland, Bill, (T), Illinois, 1947	10.00	30.00
McPherson, Forrest, (T), Nebraska, 1943-45	10.00	30.00
Meade, Mike, (FB), Penn State, 1982-83	3.00	10.00
Meilinger, Steve, (E), Kentucky, 1958-60	10.00	25.00
Melka, James, (LB), Wisconsin, 1987	3.00	10.00
Mendenhall, Ken, (C), Oklahoma, 1970	4.00	10.00
Mendoza, Ruben, (G), Wayne State, 1986	3.00	10.00
Mercein, Chuck, (B), Yale, 1967-69	8.00	25.00
Mercer, Mike, (K), Northern Arizona, 1968-69	5.00	12.00
Merrill, Casey, (DE), California-Davis, 1979-83	3.00	10.00
Merrill, Mark, (LB), Minnesota, 1982	3.00	10.00
Merriweather, Mike, (LB), Pacific, 1993	3.00	10.00
Mestnik, Frank, (B), Marquette, 1963	8.00	25.00
Meyer, Jim, (T), Illinois State, 1987	3.00	10.00
Michaels, Walt, (G), Washington & Lee, 1951	10.00	30.00

Player/Position/College/Years with Packers   *Price Range*

Michalske, Mike, (G), Penn State, (HOF), 1929-37 ....25.00   150.00

Mickens, Terry, (WR), Florida A&M, 1994......................................3.00   10.00

Middleton, Terdell, (RB), Memphis State, 1977-81 ....4.00   12.00

Midler, Lou, (G), Minnesota, 1941 ....10.00   30.00

Mihajlovick, Lou, (B), Indiana, 1954 ....8.00   25.00

Miketinac, Nick, (G), St. Norbert, 1937 ....20.00   45.00

Milan, Don, (QB), Cal Poly-San Luis Obispo, 1975 ....4.00   10.00

Millard, Keith, (DE), Washington State, 1992 ....3.00   10.00

Miller, Charles, (C), Purdue, 1938..20.00   35.00

Miller, Don, (B), Wisconsin, 1941-42 ....15.00   35.00

Miller, Don, (B), Southern Methodist, 1954....................................10.00   30.00

Miller, John, (T), Boston College, 1960 ....10.00   20.00

Miller, John, (LB), Mississippi State, 1987 ....3.00   10.00

Miller, Mark, (QB), Bowling Green, 1980 ....3.00   10.00

Miller, Paul, (B), South Dakota, 1936-38....................................20.00   45.00

Miller, Tom, (E), Hampden-Sydney, 1946 ....15.00   35.00

Mills, Tom, (B), Penn State, 1922-23 ....25.00   65.00

Milton, Tom, (E), Lake Forest, 1924 ....25.00   60.00

Minick, Paul, (G), Iowa, 1928-29 ....25.00   55.00

Mitchell, Charles, (B), Tulsa, 1946...15.00   35.00

Mitchell, Roland, (CB/S), Texas Tech, 1991-94 ....3.00   10.00

Moffitt, Mike, (WR), Fresno State, 1986......................................3.00   10.00

Moje, Dick, (E), Loyola (Calif.), 1951 ....10.00   30.00

Molenda, Bo, (B), Michigan, 1929-32...25.00   65.00

Monaco, Ron, (LB), South Carolina, 1987 ....3.00   10.00

Monnett, Bob, (B), Michigan State, 1933-38 ....20.00   45.00

Monroe, Henry, (DB), Mississippi State, 1979.................................4.00   10.00

Moore, Allen, (E), Texas A&M, 1939..20.00   45.00

Moore, Blake, (C/G), Wooster, 1984-85 ....3.00   10.00

Moore, Brent, (DE), USC, 1987 ....3.00   10.00

Moore, Rich, (DT), Villanova, 1969-70 ....4.00   12.00

Moore, Tom, (B), Vanderbilt, 1960-65..10.00   25.00

Moran, Rich, (G), San Diego State, 1985-93...................................4.00   10.00

Moresco, Tim, (DB), Syracuse, 1977 ....4.00   10.00

Morgan, Anthony, (WR), Tennessee, 1993-95....................................3.00   12.00

Morris, Jim Bob, (DB), Kansas State, 1987....................................3.00   10.00

Player/Position/College/Years with Packers	*Price Range*	
Morris, Larry, (RB), Syracuse, 1987	3.00	10.00
Morris, Lee, (WR), Oklahoma, 1987	3.00	10.00
Morrissey, Jim, (LB), Michigan State, 1993	3.00	10.00
Moselle, Dom, (B), Superior State, 1951-52	10.00	30.00
Mosley, Russ, (B), Alabama, 1945-46	15.00	35.00
Moss, Perry, (B), Illinois, 1948	15.00	35.00
Mott, Joe, (LB), Iowa, 1993	3.00	10.00
Mott, Norm, (B), Georgia, 1933	20.00	40.00
Mullen, Roderick, (CB), Grambling, 1995	3.00	10.00
Mulleneaux, Carl, (E), Utah State, 1938-41, 1945-46	20.00	45.00
Mulleneaux, Lee, (T), Northern Arizona, 1938	20.00	40.00
Murphy, Mark, (S), West Liberty State, 1980-85, 1987-91	4.00	12.00
Murray, Dick, (T), Marquette, 1921-24	25.00	75.00

N

Nadolney, Romanus, (G), Notre Dame, 1922	25.00	65.00
Nash, Tom, (E), Georgia, 1928-32	25.00	55.00
Neal, Ed, (G/C), Tulane, 1945-51	20.00	45.00
Neal, Frankie, (WR), Fort Hays State, 1987	3.00	10.00
Neill, Bill, (NT), Pittsburgh, 1984	3.00	10.00
Nelson, Bob, (NT), Miami, 1988-90	3.00	10.00
Neville, Tom, (T/G), Fresno State, 1986-88, 1992	3.00	10.00
Newsome, Craig, (CB), Arizona State, 1995-	10.00	20.00
Nichols, Ham, (G), Rice, 1951	10.00	30.00
Niemann, Walt, (C), Michigan, 1922-24	25.00	55.00
Nitschke, Ray, (LB), Illinois, (HOF), 1958-72	15.00	35.00
Nix, Doyle, (B), Southern Methodist, 1955	10.00	30.00
Nixon, Fred, (WR), Oklahoma, 1980-81	3.00	10.00
Noble, Brian, (LB), Arizona State, 1985-93	4.00	12.00
Noonan, Danny, (NT), Nebraska, 1992	3.00	10.00
Norgard, Al, (E), Stanford, 1934	20.00	45.00
Norseth, Mike, (QB), Kansas, 1990	3.00	10.00
Norton, Jerry, (DB), Southern Methodist, 1963-64	8.00	20.00
Norton, Marty, (B), Carleton, 1925-28	25.00	65.00
Nussbaumer, Bob, (B), Michigan, 1946	15.00	40.00
Nuzum, Rick, (C), Kentucky, 1978	4.00	10.00
Nystrom, Lee, (T), McAlester, 1973-74	4.00	10.00

Player/Position/College/Years with Packers	Price Range	

O

Oakes, Bill, (T), Haskell, 1921	25.00	75.00
Oates, Brad, (T), Brigham Young, 1981	3.00	10.00
Oats, Carleton, (DT), Florida A&M, 1973	4.00	10.00
O'Boyle, Harry, (B), Notre Dame, 1928-29, 1932	25.00	65.00
O'Connor, Bob, (T), Stanford, 1935	20.00	45.00
Odom, Steve, (WR), Utah, 1974-79	4.00	12.00
O'Donahue, Pat, (E), Wisconsin, 1955	8.00	25.00
O'Donnell, Dick, (E), Minnesota, 1924-30	25.00	65.00
Odson, Urban, (T), Minnesota, 1946-49	15.00	45.00
Oglesby, Alfred, (NT), Houston, 1992	3.00	10.00
Ohlgren, Earl, (E), Minnesota, 1942	15.00	40.00
Okoniewski, Steve, (DT), Montana, 1974-75	4.00	10.00
Oliver, Muhammad, (CB), Oregon, 1993	3.00	10.00
Olsen, Ralph, (E), Utah, 1949	15.00	35.00
Olsonoski, Larry, (G), Minnesota, 1948-49	15.00	35.00
O'Malley, Jack, (T), USC, 1970	4.00	12.00
O'Malley, Tom, (QB), Cincinnati, 1950	8.00	25.00
O'Neil, Ed, (LB), Penn State, 1980	3.00	10.00
Orlich, Dan, (E), Nevada, 1949-51	10.00	25.00
Osborn, Dave, (RB), North Dakota, 1976	4.00	10.00
O'Steen, Dwayne, (CB), San Jose State, 1983-84	3.00	10.00
Owens, Henry, (G), Lake Forest, 1922	25.00	65.00

P

Palumbo, Sam, (G), Notre Dame, 1957	8.00	25.00
Pannell, Ernie, (T), Texas A&M, 1941-42, 1945	15.00	40.00
Pape, Orrin, (B), Iowa, 1930	25.00	60.00
Papit, John, (B), Virginia, 1953	8.00	25.00
Parilli, Babe, (QB), Kentucky, 1952-53, 1956-58	12.00	30.00
Parker, Freddie, (RB), Miss, Valley State, 1987	3.00	10.00
Paskett, Keith, (WR), Western Kentucky, 1987	3.00	10.00
Paskvan, George, (B), Wisconsin, 1941	15.00	40.00
Pass, Randy, (LB), Georgia Tech, 1978	4.00	10.00
Patrick, Frank, (QB), Nebraska, 1970-72	4.00	12.00

Player/Position/College/Years with Packers	_Price Range_	
Patterson, Shawn, (DE), Arizona State, 1988-91, 1993	3.00	10.00
Patton, Ricky, (B), Jackson State, 1979	20.00	45.00
Paulekas, Tony, (C), Washington and Jefferson, 1936	20.00	45.00
Paup, Bryce, (LB), Northern Iowa, 1990-94	5.00	20.00
Payne, Ken, (WR), Langston, 1974-77	4.00	12.00
Pearson, Lindell, (B), Oklahoma, 1952	8.00	25.00
Peay, Francis, (T), Missouri, 1968-72	5.00	15.00
Pelfrey, Ray, (E), East Kentucky State, 1951-52	8.00	25.00
Perkins, Don, (B), Platteville State Teachers, 1943-45	15.00	40.00
Perko, Tom, (LB), Pittsburgh, 1976	4.00	10.00
Perry, Claude, (T), Alabama, 1927-35	25.00	65.00
Pesonen, Dick, (DB), Minnesota-Duluth, 1960	10.00	25.00
Peterson, Les, (E), Texas, 1932-35	20.00	45.00
Peterson, Phil, (B), Wisconsin, 1932	20.00	45.00
Peterson, Ray, (B), San Francisco, 1937	20.00	45.00
Petitbon, John, (B), Notre Dame, 1957	8.00	25.00
Petway, David, (S), Northern Illinois, 1981	3.00	10.00
Pickens, Bruce, (CB), Nebraska, 1993	3.00	10.00
Pisarkiewicz, Steve, (QB), Missouri, 1980	3.00	10.00
Pitts, Elijah, (B), Philander Smith, 1961-69, 1971	10.00	25.00
Pitts, Ron, (CB), UCLA, 1988-90	4.00	12.00
Ploeger, Kurt, (DE), Gustavus Adolphus, 1986	3.00	10.00
Pointer, John, (LB), Vanderbilt, 1987	3.00	10.00
Pope, Bucky, (E), Catawba, 1968	4.00	12.00
Powers, Sam, (G), Northern Michigan, 1921	25.00	75.00
Prather, Guy, (LB), Grambling, 1981-85	3.00	10.00
Pregulman, Merv, (G), Pittsburgh, 1957	8.00	25.00
Prescott, Ace, (E), Hardin-Simmons, 1946	15.00	40.00
Priatko, Bill, (G), Pittsburgh, 1957	8.00	25.00
Prior, Mike, (S), Illinois State, 1993-	10.00	25.00
Pritko, Steve, (E), Villanova, 1949-50	10.00	30.00
Prokop, Joe, (P), Cal Poly-San Luis Obispo, 1985	3.00	10.00
Provo, Fred, (B), Washington, 1948	10.00	30.00
Psaltis, Jim, (B), USC, 1954	8.00	25.00
Purdy, Pid, (B), Beloit, 1926-27	25.00	60.00
Pureifory, Dave, (DL), Eastern Michigan, 1972-77	4.00	12.00

Player/Position/College/Years with Packers	*Price Range*	
Purnell, Frank, (B), Alcorn A&M, 1957	8.00	25.00
Putman, Earl, (C), Arizona State, 1957	8.00	25.00

Q

Quatse, Jess, (T), Pittsburgh, 1933	20.00	45.00
Query, Jeff, (WR), Millikin, 1989-91	3.00	10.00
Quinian, Bill, (E), Michigan State, 1959-62	8.00	25.00

R

Radick, Ken, (E), Marquette, 1930-31	20.00	55.00
Rafferty, Vince, (C), Colorado, 1987	3.00	10.00
Randolph, Al, (DB), Iowa, 1971	4.00	10.00
Randolph, Terry, (DB), American International, 1977	3.00	10.00
Ranspot, Keith, (E), Southern Methodist, 1942	15.00	40.00
Rash, Louis, (DB), Mississippi Valley State, 1987	3.00	12.00
Ray, Baby, (T), Vanderbilt, 1938-48	20.00	55.00
Redick, Cornelius, (WR), Cal St.-Fullerton, 1987	3.00	10.00
Regnier, Pete, (B), Minnesota, 1922	25.00	65.00
Reichardt, Bill, (B), Iowa, 1952	8.00	25.00
Reid, Floyd, (B), Georgia, 1950-56	10.00	25.00
Renner, Bill, (P), Virginia Tech, 1986-87	3.00	10.00
Rhodemyre, Jay, (C), Kentucky, 1948-52	15.00	35.00
Rice, Allen, (RB), Baylor, 1991	3.00	10.00
Richard, Gary, (DB), Pittsburgh, 1988	3.00	10.00
Riddick, Ray, (E), Fordham, 1940-42, 1946	15.00	35.00
Ringo, Jim, (C), Syracuse, (HOF), 1953-63	10.00	30.00
Risher, Alan, (QB), Louisiana State, 1987	3.00	10.00
Rison, Andre, (WR), Michigan State, 1995	10.00	25.00
Roach, John, (QB), South Methodist, 1961-63	10.00	25.00
Robbins, Tootie, (T), East Carolina, 1992-93	3.00	10.00
Roberts, Bill, (B), Dartmouth, 1956	8.00	25.00
Robinson, Bill, (B), Lincoln (Pa.), 1952	8.00	25.00
Robinson, Dave, (LB), Penn State, 1963-72	10.00	25.00
Robison, Tom, (G), Texas A&M, 1987	3.00	10.00
Roche, Alden, (DT), Southern University, 1971-76	4.00	10.00

Player/Position/College/Years with Packers	*Price Range*	
Rodgers, Del, (RB), Utah, 1982, 1984	3.00	10.00
Rohrig, Herman, (B), Nebraska, 1941, 1946-47	15.00	40.00
Roller, Dave, (DT), Kentucky, 1975-78	4.00	12.00
Romine, Al, (E), Alabama, 1955, 1958	8.00	25.00
Rosatti, Roman, (T), Michigan, 1924, 1926-27	25.00	65.00
Rose, Al, (E), Texas, 1932-36	20.00	45.00
Rose, Bob, (C), Ripon, 1926	25.00	55.00
Rosenow, Gus, (B), Wisconsin, 1921	25.00	75.00
Roskie, Ken, (B), South Carolina, 1948	15.00	35.00
Ross, Dan, (TE), Northeastern, 1986	3.00	10.00
Rote, Tobin, (QB), Rice, 1950-56	10.00	30.00
Rowser, John, (DB), Michigan, 1967-69	8.00	25.00
Rubens, Larry, (C), Montana State, 1982-83	3.00	10.00
Rubley, T.J., (QB), Tulsa, 1995	3.00	10.00
Rudzinski, Paul, (LB), Michigan State, 1978-81	3.00	10.00
Ruettgers, Ken, (T), USC, 1985-95	4.00	15.00
Ruetz, Howard, (T), Loras, 1951-53	8.00	25.00
Rule, Gordon, (DB), Dartmouth, 1968-69	4.00	10.00
Rush, Clive, (E), Miami (Ohio), 1953	8.00	25.00
Ruzich, Steve, (G), Ohio State, 1952-54	8.00	25.00

S

Salem, Harvey, (T), California, 1992	3.00	10.00
Salsbury, Jim, (G), UCLA, 1957-58	8.00	25.00
Sample, Chuck, (B), Toledo, 1942, 1945	15.00	35.00
Sampson, Howard, (DB), Arkansas, 1978-79	4.00	10.00
Sams, Ron, (G), Pittsburgh, 1983	3.00	10.00
Sandifer, Dan, (B), Louisiana State, 1952-53	8.00	25.00
Sandusky, John, (T), Villanova, 1956	8.00	25.00
Sarafiny, Al, (C), St. Edward's, 1933	20.00	35.00
Sauer, George, (B), Nebraska, 1935-37	20.00	45.00
Saunders, Russ, (B), USC, 1931	25.00	50.00
Scales, Hurles, (DB), North Texas State, 1975	4.00	10.00
Schammel, Fran, (G), Iowa, 1937	20.00	40.00
Scherer, Bernie, (E), Nebraska, 1936-38	20.00	45.00
Schlinkman, Walt, (B), Texas Tech, 1946-50	15.00	35.00

Player/Position/College/Years with Packers

	Price Range	
Schmaehl, Art, (B), no college, 1921	25.00	75.00
Schmidt, George, (C), Lewis, 1952-53	8.00	25.00
Schmitt, John, (C), Hofstra, 1974	4.00	10.00
Schneidman, Herm, (B), Iowa, 1935-39	20.00	45.00
Schoemann, Roy, (C), Marquette, 1938	20.00	40.00
Schroeder, Bill, (WR), Wisconsin-LaCrosse, 1994-	3.00	10.00
Schroll, Chuck, (B), Louisiana State, 1951	8.00	25.00
Schuette, Carl, (B), Marquette, 1950-51	8.00	25.00
Schuh, Jeff, (LB), Minnesota, 1986	3.00	10.00
Schuh, Harry, (T), Memphis State, 1974	4.00	10.00
Schultz, Charles, (T), Minnesota, 1939-41	20.00	40.00
Schwammel, Ade, (T), Oregon State, 1934-37, 1943-44	20.00	45.00
Scott, Patrick, (WR), Grambling, 1987-88	3.00	10.00
Scott, Randy, (LB), Alabama, 1981-86	4.00	10.00
Scribner, Bucky, (P), Kansas, 1983-84	3.00	10.00
Secord, Joe, (C), no college, 1922	25.00	65.00
Seeman, George, (E), Nebraska, 1940	15.00	35.00
Seibold, Champ, (T), Wisconsin, 1934-41	20.00	45.00
Self, Clarence, (B), Wisconsin, 1952, 1954-55	8.00	25.00
Serini, Wash, (G), Kentucky, 1952	8.00	25.00
Shanley, Jim, (B), Oregon, 1958	8.00	25.00
Sharpe, Sterling, (WR), South Carolina, 1988-94	10.00	25.00
Shelly, Dexter, (B), Texas, 1932-33	15.00	45.00
Shield, Joe, (QB), Trinity (Conn.) College, 1985-86	3.00	10.00
Shirey, Fred, (T), Nebraska, 1940	15.00	40.00
Shumate, Mark, (DE), Wisconsin, 1985	3.00	10.00
Sikahema, Vai, (RB/KR), Brigham Young, 1991	3.00	10.00
Simmons, Davie, (LB), North Carolina, 1979-80	3.00	10.00
Simmons, John, (DB), Southern Methodist, 1986	3.00	10.00
Simmons, Wayne, (LB), Clemson, 1993-	10.00	25.00
Simpkins, Ron, (LB), Michigan, 1988	3.00	10.00
Simpson, Nate, (RB), Tennessee, 1977-79	4.00	10.00
Simpson, Travis, (C), Oklahoma, 1987	3.00	10.00
Sims, Joe, (T/G), Nebraska, 1992-95	3.00	10.00
Singletary, Reggie, (T), North Carolina State, 1991	3.00	10.00
Skaugstad, Daryle, (NT), California, 1983	3.00	10.00

Player/Position/College/Years with Packers   *Price Range*

Player/Position/College/Years with Packers		
Skeate, Gil, (B), Gonzaga, 1927	25.00	55.00
Skibinski, Joe, (G), Purdue, 1955-56	8.00	25.00
Skinner, Gerald, (T), Arkansas, 1978	4.00	10.00
Skoglund, Bob, (E), Notre Dame, 1947	15.00	35.00
Skoronski, Bob, (T), Indiana, 1956, 1959-68	10.00	25.00
Sleight, Elmer, (T), Indiana, 1930-31	20.00	55.00
Smith, Barry, (WR), Florida State, 1973-75	4.00	12.00
Smith, Barty, (RB), Richmond, 1974-80	4.00	12.00
Smith, Ben, (E), Alabama, 1933	20.00	45.00
Smith, Blane, (G), Purdue, 1977	4.00	10.00
Smith, Bruce, (B), Minnesota, 1945-48	15.00	35.00
Smith, Donnell, (DE), Southern University, 1971	4.00	10.00
Smith, Earl, (T), Ripon, 1922	25.00	65.00
Smith, Ed, (B), New York University, 1971	4.00	10.00
Smith, Ernie, (T), USC, 1935-37, 1939	20.00	50.00
Smith, Jerry, (G), Wisconsin, 1956	8.00	25.00
Smith, Ollie, (WR), Tennessee State, 1976-77	4.00	10.00
Smith, Oscar, (B), Texas Mines, 1948-49	15.00	35.00
Smith, Perry, (DB), Colorado State, 1973-76	4.00	10.00
Smith, Red, (G), Notre Dame, 1927-29	25.00	65.00
Smith, Rex, (E), Wisconsin Teachers, 1922	25.00	65.00
Smith, Warren, (C), Carleton, 1921	25.00	75.00
Smith, Wes, (WR), East Texas State, 1987	3.00	10.00
Snelling, Ken, (B), UCLA, 1947	15.00	35.00
Snider, Malcolm (OL), Stanford, 1972-74	4.00	10.00
Sorenson, Glen, (G), Utah State, 1943-45	15.00	45.00
Spagnola, John, (TE), Yale, 1989	3.00	10.00
Sparlis, Al, (G), UCLA, 1947	15.00	35.00
Spears, Ron, (DE), San Diego State, 1983	3.00	10.00
Spencer, Joe, (T), Oklahoma A&M, 1950-51	8.00	25.00
Spencer, Ollie, (T), Kansas, 1957-58	8.00	25.00
Spilis, John, (WR), Northern Illinois, 1969-71	4.00	12.00
Spinks, Jack, (G), Alcorn A&M, 1955-56	8.00	25.00
Sproul, Dennis, (QB), Arizona State, 1978	4.00	10.00
Stachowicz, Ray, (P), Michigan State, 1981-82	3.00	10.00
Staggers, Jon, (WR), Missouri, 1972-74	4.00	10.00

Player/Position/College/Years with Packers · Price Range

Player/Position/College/Years with Packers		
Stahlman, Dick, (E), Chicago, 1931-32	20.00	50.00
Stanley, Walter, (WR), Missouri, 1972-74	4.00	10.00
Stansauk, Don, (T), Denver, 1950-51	8.00	25.00
Starch, Ken, (RB), Wisconsin, 1976	4.00	10.00
Staroba, Paul, (WR), Michigan, 1973	4.00	10.00
Starr, Bart, (QB), Alabama, (HOF), 1956-71	25.00	55.00
Starret, Ben, (B), St. Mary's, 1942-45	15.00	35.00
Steen, Frank, (E), Rice, 1939	20.00	45.00
Steiner, Rebel, (E), Alabama, 1950-51	8.00	25.00
Stenerud, Jan, (K), Montana State, (HOF), 1980-83	10.00	25.00
Stephen, Scott, (LB), Arizona State, 1987-91	3.00	10.00
Stephens, John, (RB), Northwestern (La.) State, 1993	3.00	10.00
Stephenson, Dave, (G), West Virginia, 1951-54	8.00	25.00
Sterling, John, (RB), Central Oklahoma, 1987	3.00	10.00
Stevens, Bill, (QB), Texas-El Paso, 1968-69	4.00	12.00
Stewart, Steve, (LB), Minnesota, 1979	3.00	10.00
Stills, Ken, (DB), Wisconsin, 1985-89	3.00	10.00
Stokes, Tim, (T), Oregon, 1978-82	3.00	10.00
Stonebraker, John, (E), USC, 1942	15.00	35.00
Strickland, Fred, (LB), Purdue, 1994-95	3.00	10.00
Sturgeon, Lyle, (T), North Dakota State, 1937	20.00	45.00
Sullivan, Carl, (DE), San Jose State, 1987	3.00	10.00
Sullivan, Walter, (G), Beloit, 1921	25.00	75.00
Summerhays, Bob, (B), Utah, 1949-51	10.00	30.00
Summers, Don, (TE), Boise State, 1987	3.00	10.00
Sutton, Mickey, (CB), Montana, 1989	3.00	10.00
Svendsen, Earl, (C), Minnesota, 1937-40	15.00	40.00
Svendsen, George, (C), Minnesota, 1935-41	20.00	50.00
Swanke, Karl, (T/C), Boston College, 1980-86	4.00	10.00
Switzer, Veryl, (B), Kansas State, 1954-55	8.00	25.00
Sydney, Harry, (FB), Kansas, 1992	5.00	15.00
Symank, John, (B), Florida, 1957-62	10.00	25.00
Szafaryn, Len, (T), North Carolina, 1950, 1953-56	8.00	25.00

T

Tagge, Jerry, (QB), Nebraska, 1972-74	4.00	12.00
Tassos, Damon, (G), Texas A&M, 1947-49	15.00	35.00
Taugher, Claude, (B), Marquette, 1922	25.00	65.00

Player/Position/College/Years with Packers   Price Range

Player/Position/College/Years with Packers	Low	High
Taylor, Aaron, (G), Notre Dame, 1995-	10.00	25.00
Taylor, Cliff, (RB), Memphis State, 1976	4.00	12.00
Taylor, Jim, (B), Louisiana State, (HOF), 1958-66	15.00	35.00
Taylor, Kitrick, (WR), Washington State, 1992	3.00	10.00
Taylor, Lenny, (WR), Tennessee, 1984	3.00	10.00
Teague, George, (S), Alabama, 1993-95	4.00	12.00
Temp, Jim, (E), Wisconsin, 1957-60	8.00	25.00
Tenner, Bob, (E), Minnesota, 1935	20.00	40.00
Teteak, Deral (LB/G), Wisconsin, 1952-56	8.00	25.00
Thomas, Ben, (DE), Auburn, 1986	3.00	10.00
Thomas, Ike, (DB), Bishop College, 1972-73	4.00	12.00
Thomas, Lavale, (RB), Fresno State, 1987-88	3.00	10.00
Thomason, Bob, (B), Virginia Military, 1951	8.00	25.00
Thomason, Jeff, (TE), Oregon, 1995-	10.00	25.00
Thompson, Arland, (G), Baylor, 1981	3.00	10.00
Thompson, Aundra, (WR), East Texas State, 1977-81	3.00	10.00
Thompson, Clarence, (B), Minnesota, 1939	20.00	45.00
Thompson, Darrell, (RB), Minnesota, 1990-94	3.00	10.00
Thompson, John, (TE), Utah State, 1979-82	3.00	10.00
Thurston, Fred, (G), Valparaiso, 1959-67	10.00	25.00
Timberlake, George, (C), USC, 1955	8.00	25.00
Timmerman, Adam, (G), South Dakota State, 1995-	10.00	25.00
Tinker, Gerald, (WR), Kent State, 1975	4.00	10.00
Tinsley, Pete, (G), Georgia, 1938-45	15.00	40.00
Toburen, Nelson, (LB), Wichita State, 1961-62	10.00	25.00
Tollefson, Chuck, (G), Iowa, 1944-46	15.00	35.00
Tomczak, Mike, (QB), Ohio State, 1991	4.00	12.00
Toner, Tom, (LB), Idaho State, 1973-77	4.00	12.00
Tonnemaker, Clayton, (LB/C), Minnesota, 1950, 1953-54	8.00	25.00
Torkelson, Eric, (RB), Connecticut, 1974-79, 1981	5.00	14.00
Traylor, Keith, (LB), Central Oklahoma, 1993	3.00	10.00
Troup, Bill, (QB), South Carolina, 1980	3.00	10.00
Tuaolo, Esera, (NT/DE), Oregon State, 1991-92	3.00	10.00
Tullis, Walter, (WR), Delaware State, 1978-79	3.00	10.00
Tunnell, Emlen, (S), Iowa, (HOF), 1959-61	15.00	35.00
Turner, Maurice, (RB), Utah State, 1985	3.00	10.00

Player/Position/College/Years with Packers	_Price Range_	
Turner, Rich, (DT), Oklahoma, 1981-83	3.00	10.00
Turner, Wylie, (DB), Angelo State, 1979-80	3.00	10.00
Turpin, Miles, (LB), California, 1986	3.00	10.00
Tuttle, Dick, (E), Minnesota, 1927	20.00	65.00
Twedell, Fran, (G), Minnesota, 1939	20.00	45.00

U

Uecker, Keith, (G/T), Auburn, 1984-85, 1987-88, 1990-91	3.00	10.00
Uram, Andy, (B), Minnesota, 1938-43	20.00	45.00
Urban, Alex, (E), South Carolina, 1941, 1944-45	15.00	40.00
Usher, Ed, (B), Michigan, 1922-24	25.00	65.00

V

Vairo, Dominic, (E), Notre Dame, 1935	20.00	40.00
VanderSea, Phil, (B/LB), Massachusetts, 1966, 1968-70	10.00	25.00
Van Dyke, Bruce, (G), Missouri, 1974-76	4.00	10.00
Van Every, Hal, (B), Minnesota, 1940-41	15.00	35.00
Vanoy, Vernon, (DL), Kansas, 1972	4.00	12.00
Van Sickle, Clyde, (C), Arkansas, 1923-33	20.00	40.00
VantHull, Fred, (G), Minnesota, 1942	15.00	35.00
Van Valkenburg, Pete, (RB), Brigham Young, 1974	4.00	10.00
Vataha, Randy, (WR), Stanford, 1977	4.00	10.00
Vegara, George, (E), Notre Dame, 1925	25.00	65.00
Viengrad, Alan, (T), East Texas State, 1986-87, 1989-90	3.00	10.00
Vereen, Carl, (T), Georgia Tech, 1957	8.00	25.00
Viaene, David, (T), Minnesota-Deluth, 1992	3.00	10.00
Villanucci, Vince, (NT), Bowling Green, 1987	3.00	10.00
Vogds, Evan, (G), Wisconsin, 1948-49	15.00	35.00
Voss, Walter, (E), Detroit, 1924	25.00	45.00

W

Wagner, Bryan, (P), Cal State Northridge, 1992-93	3.00	10.00
Wagner, Buffton, (B), Northern Michigan, 1921	25.00	75.00
Wagner, Steve, (DB), Wisconsin, 1976-79	4.00	10.00
Walker, Cleo (C/LB), Louisville, 1970	4.00	10.00

Player/Position/College/Years with Packers	_Price Range_	
Walker, Malcom, (C), Rice, 1970	4.00	10.00
Walker, Randy, (P), Northwestern (La.) State, 1974	4.00	10.00
Walker, Sammy, (CB), Texas Tech, 1993	3.00	10.00
Walker, Val Joe, (B), South Methodist, 1953-56	8.00	25.00
Wallace, Calvin, (DE), West Virginia Tech, 1987	8.00	25.00
Walsh, Ward, (RB), Tennessee, 1972-73	4.00	12.00
Washington, Chuck, (DB), Arkansas, 1987	3.00	10.00
Watts, Elbert, (RB), USC, 1986	3.00	10.00
Weathers, Clarence, (WR), Delaware State, 1990-91	3.00	10.00
Weatherwax, Jim, (T), Cal St.-LA, 1966-69	10.00	25.00
Weaver, Gary, (LB), Fresno State, 1928	4.00	10.00
Webb, Chuck, (RB), Tennessee, 1991	3.00	10.00
Webber, Howard, (E), Kansas State, 1928	25.00	60.00
Webster, Tim, (K), Arkansas, 1971	4.00	10.00
Weddington, Mike, (LB), Oklahoma, 1986-90	3.00	10.00
Wehba, Ray, (E), USC, 1944	15.00	40.00
Weigel, Lee, (RB), Wisconsin Eau-Claire, 1987	3.00	10.00
Weisgerber, Dick, (B), Williamette, 1938-40, 1942	25.00	40.00
Weishuhn, Clayton, (LB), Angelo State, 1987	3.00	10.00
Wellman, Mike, (C), Kansas, 1979-80	3.00	10.00
Wells, Don, (E), Georgia, 1946-49	15.00	35.00
Wells, Terry, (RB), Southern Mississippi, 1975	4.00	10.00
West, Ed, (TE), Auburn, 1984-94	5.00	12.00
West, Pat, (B), USC, 1948	15.00	35.00
Wheeler, Lyle, (E), Ripon, 1921-23	25.00	75.00
Whitaker, Bill, (DB), Missouri, 1981-82	3.00	10.00
White, Adrian, (S), Florida, 1992	3.00	10.00
White, Gene, (B), Georgia, 1954	8.00	25.00
White, Reggie, (DE), Tennessee, 1993-	20.00	55.00
White, Russell, (RB), California, 1995	3.00	10.00
Whitehurst, David, (QB), Furman, 1977-83	4.00	12.00
Whittenton Jesse, (B), Texas Western, 1958-64	10.00	25.00
Widby, Ron, (P), Tennessee, 1972	4.00	12.00
Widell, Doug, (G), Boston College, 1993	3.00	10.00
Wildung, Dick, (T), Minnesota, 1946-51, 1953	8.00	25.00
Wilkins, Gabe, (DE/DT), Gardner-Webb, 1994	10.00	25.00

Player/Position/College/Years with Packers		Price Range	
Wilkins, Ted, (E), Indiana, 1925	25.00	65.00
Willhite, Kevin, (RB), Oregon, 1987	3.00	10.00
Williams, A.D., (E), Pacific, 1959	8.00	25.00
Williams, Brian, (LB), USC, 1995-	10.00	25.00
Williams, Clarence, (DE), Prairie View A&M, 1970-77	4.00	12.00
Williams, Delvin, (RB), Kansas, 1981	3.00	10.00
Williams, Dick, (B), Wisconsin, 1921	25.00	75.00
Williams, Howard, (B), Howard, 1962-63	10.00	25.00
Williams, Kevin, (RB), UCLA, 1993	3.00	10.00
Williams, Mark, (LB), Ohio State, 1994	3.00	10.00
Williams, Perry, (RB), Purdue, 1969-73	4.00	12.00
Williams, Travis, (HB), Arizona State, 1967-70	10.00	30.00
Willis, James, (LB), Auburn, 1993-94	3.00	10.00
Wilner, Jeff, (TE), Wesleyan (Conn.), 1994-	10.00	25.00
Wilson, Ben, (FB), USC, 1967	10.00	25.00
Wilson, Charles, (WR), Memphis State, 1990-91	3.00	10.00
Wilson, Faye, (B), Texas A&M, 1931	20.00	60.00
Wilson, Gene, (E), Southern Methodist, 1947-48	15.00	35.00
Wilson, John, (B), Dubuque, 1939	20.00	50.00
Wilson, Marcus, (RB), Virginia, 1992-95	3.00	10.00
Wilson, Milt, (T), Wisconsin Teachers, 1921	25.00	75.00
Wilson, Ray, (S), New Mexico, 1994	3.00	10.00
Wimberly, Abner, (E), Louisiana State, 1950-52	8.00	25.00
Wingle, Blake, (G), UCLA, 1985	3.00	10.00
Wingo, Rich, (LB), Alabama, 1979, 1981-84	3.00	10.00
Winkler, Francis, (DE), Memphis State, 1968-69	4.00	12.00
Winkler, Randy, (G), Tarlton State, 1971	4.00	12.00
Winslow, Paul, (RB), North Carolina College, 1960	10.00	25.00
Winter, Blaise, (DL), Syracuse, 1988-90	3.00	10.00
Winters, Arnold, (T), no college, 1945	15.00	35.00
Winters, Chet, (RB), Oklahoma, 1983	3.00	10.00
Winters, Frank, (C/G), Western Illinois, 1992-	10.00	25.00
Winther, Wimpy, (C), Mississippi, 1971	4.00	10.00
Withrow, Cal, (C), Kentucky, 1971-73	4.00	12.00
Witte, Earl, (B), Gustavus Adolphus, 1934	15.00	35.00
Wizbicki, Alex, (B), Holy Cross, 1950	10.00	25.00

Player/Position/College/Years with Packers	_Price Range_	
Wood, Willie, (S), USC, (HOF), 1960-71	12.00	30.00
Woodin, Whitey, (G), Marquette, 1922-31	25.00	75.00
Woods, Jerry, (S), Northern Michigan, 1990	3.00	10.00
Woodside, Keith, (RB), Texas A&M, 1988-91	4.00	10.00
Workman, Vince, (RB), Ohio State, 1989-92	4.00	10.00
Wortman, Keith, (G), Nebraska, 1972-75	4.00	12.00
Wright, Randy, (QB), Wisconsin, 1984-88	4.00	12.00
Wright, Steve, (T), Alabama, 1964-66	10.00	25.00
Wunsch, Harry, (G), Notre Dame, 1934	20.00	35.00

Y

Young, Bill, (G), Ohio State, 1929	25.00	75.00
Young, Glenn, (B), Purdue, 1956-57	8.00	25.00
Young, Paul, (C), Oklahoma, 1933	10.00	35.00
Young, Steve, (T), Colorado, 1979	3.00	10.00

Z

Zarnas, Gus, (G), Ohio State, 1939-40	20.00	45.00
Zatkoff, Roger, (LB), Michigan, 1953-56	8.00	25.00
Zeller, Joe, (G), Indiana, 1932	20.00	40.00
Zendejas, Max, (K), Arizona, 1987-88	3.00	10.00
Zeno, Lance, (C), UCLA, 1993	3.00	10.00
Zimmerman, Don, (WR), Northeast La, 1976	4.00	10.00
Zoll, Carl, (G), no college, 1921-22	25.00	75.00
Zoll, Dick, (G), Indiana, 1939	20.00	45.00
Zoll, Martin, (G), no college, 1921	25.00	75.00
Zorn, Jim, (QB), Cal Poly-Pomona, 1985	5.00	15.00
Zuidmulder, Dave, (B), St. Ambrose, 1929-31	25.00	75.00
Zupek, Al, (E), Lawrence, 1946	15.00	35.00
Zuver, Merle, (C), Nebraska, 1930	25.00	65.00

Team-Signed Items	Price Range Championship Year		Price Range Non-Championship Year	
1920s 750.00	2,500.00+		500.00	1,500.00+
1930s 500.00	2,000.00+		350.00	1,250.00+
1940s 450.00	1,750.00+		300.00	1,000.00+
1950s ....n/a	n/a		200.00	600.00+
1960s 500.00	2,000.00+		350.00	1,250.00+
1970s ....n/a	n/a		75.00	325.00+
1980s .... n/a	n/a		75.00	300.00+
1990s 250.00	750.00+		75.00	300.00+

Pro Football Hall of Famers

Nineteen individuals who spent most of their careers with Packers are now in the Pro Football Hall of Fame in Canton, Ohio. That's the second-most players of any club. The Chicago Bears have 24 players in the Hall of Fame. The New York Giants have 15 and the Pittsburgh Steelers and Washington Redskins have 14 each. Additionally, five players who played briefly for Packers—Len Ford, Ted Hendricks, Walt Kiesling, Jan Stenerud and Emlen Tunnell—are also in the Hall of Fame. From recent years, look for more Hall of Famers, such Hall of Fame locks like Reggie White and Brett Favre. On the list of possible Hall of Famers are Sean Jones, Mike Holmgren and LeRoy Butler. Jerry Kramer is another oft-mentioned inductee. Here are the Packers who are Hall of Famers:

- Earl L. "Curly" Lambeau, 1963
- Robert "Cal" Hubbard, 1963
- Don Hutson, 1963
- Johnny "Blood" McNally, 1963
- Clarke Hinkle, 1964
- Mike Michalske, 1964
- Arnie Herber, 1966
- Vince Lombardi, 1971
- Tony Canadeo, 1974
- Jim Taylor, 1976

- Forrest Gregg, 1977
- Bart Starr, 1977
- Ray Nitschke, 1978
- Herb Adderley, 1980
- Willie Davis, 1981
- Jim Ringo, 1981
- Paul Hornung, 1986
- Willie Wood, 1989
- Henry Jordan, 1995

Chapter 3

Banners and Flags

Banners can make a very challenging collectible. They come in a large variety of sizes, ages and designs. Banners from special events, Championships, Super Bowls, the stadium or banquets, can be very valuable. Some older banners had sewn-on lettering and designs, while most of the newer banners were usually made of canvas or cotton cloth. Most modern banners are vinyl or plastic and are much easier to obtain. Flags from the stadium or parades can be valuable. Most older flags and banners were thrown away or damaged in storage, making them difficult to find. Condition is important in estimating a banner's or a flag's price. Stains, tears, fading and holes all detract from the value.

Years	_Banners_		_Flags_	
1920s	500.00	5,000.00	300.00	1,250.00
1930s	500.00	3,000.00	250.00	1,000.00
1940s	400.00	2,000.00	200.00	750.00
1950s	300.00	1,500.00	100.00	500.00
1960s	300.00	1,500.00	75.00	500.00
1970s	100.00	500.00	50.00	350.00
1980s	75.00	200.00	25.00	150.00
1990s	50.00	150.00	15.00	100.00

Domination by a Receiver

Did you know that Don Hutson led the league in catches eight times. He was the top pass catcher from 1936-37, 1939 and 1941-45. His eight times leading the league is a record, as is five consecutive seasons. He also holds the NFL record for most seasons leading the league in receiving yardage (seven) and most consecutive years of leading in that category (four, from 1941-44).

Chapter 4

Banks

Packers banks come in many shapes and sizes. The most popular shapes are helmets, players and footballs. Ceramic football banks of the 1940s are getting difficult to find. The 1960s "Player Statue" banks have risen drastically in price during the last few years. Banks from the 1970s to the present are much easier to obtain. Modern banks are being made as a collectible; not many will be used or thrown away, so their value will likely not be great in the future. As with most collectibles, condition is important when determining a bank's price. Look for chips, cracks or repairs. The original box will add up to 25% more to a bank's value, depending on how detailed the graphic design is on the box. The following bank prices vary according to condition and desirability of the banks.

Years	*Price Range*	
1920s	50.00	200.00
1930s	45.00	150.00
1940s	40.00	125.00
1950s	30.00	100.00
1960s	25.00	100.00
1970s	20.00	65.00
1980s	15.00	45.00
1990s	10.00	35.00

Here are some specific banks and their prices:

Bank	*Price Range*	
1949, football-shaped, ceramic, 5" long	40.00	95.00
1961, football player, ceramic, 8", marked "FAK"	25.00	75.00
1973, helmet bank, plastic	15.00	30.00
1990s, Ertl cars and trucks, various models, each	25.00	45.00

Chapter 5

Banquet Items

Early Packers banquets were held at the Columbus Club in Green Bay. Banquet programs, banners, tickets, invitations, photographs and other souvenirs from 1929, 1930, 1931, 1936, 1939 and 1944 are valuable and hard to find. Starting in the early 1960s, the Elk's Club in Green Bay had an annual awards banquet. Because of the large number of NFL Hall of Fame players and coaches that attended these banquets, signed banquet items are highly prized. The Packers Hall of Fame Banquet has been giving out goblets every year since 1973. They are quite collectible and are reasonably priced. One of the nice features of many banquet items is that they are usually dated. As with all collectibles, check condition closely when making any purchases.

Columbus Club Banquet Programs

Year	Price Range (unsigned)		Price Range (signed)	
1929	50.00	150.00	300.00	1,000.00
1930	50.00	150.00	300.00	1,000.00
1931	50.00	150.00	300.00	1,000.00
1936	40.00	125.00	200.00	750.00
1939	40.00	125.00	200.00	750.00
1944	40.00	125.00	200.00	750.00

Elk Club Banquet Programs

Year	Price Range (unsigned)		Price Range (signed)	
1962	25.00	75.00	200.00	450.00
1963	25.00	75.00	150.00	300.00
1964	25.00	65.00	150.00	350.00
1965	25.00	65.00	200.00	600.00
1966	20.00	50.00	100.00	400.00
1967	10.00	35.00	50.00	150.00
1968	5.00	25.00	25.00	100.00

Packers Hall of Fame Goblets

Year	Price
1973	40.00
1974	40.00
1975	35.00
1976	35.00
1977	30.00
1978	30.00
1979	25.00
1980	25.00
1981	20.00
1982	20.00
1983	20.00
1984	20.00

Packers Hall of Fame Goblets—1973 ($40).

Packers Hall of Fame Goblets— 1993 ($15).

Chapter 6

Bobbing Head Dolls

Bobbing head dolls are very popular collectibles. They have tripled in value in the last few years. There are at least 25 different variations of Packers bobbing head dolls. They have been made from the early 1960s to the present. The 1960s dolls were made of plaster and were played with a lot. Because of this, they were often damaged. The 1970s and 1980s dolls were made out of rubber and they are much more durable. The dolls range in size from just more than 3 inches to about 15 inches.

The first Packers bobbing head doll from 1961 has a green square wood base and no "G" on the helmet. The 1962-63 bobbing head dolls have a plaster base and a "G" on the helmet. In the mid-1960s, dolls with a round gold base and toes pointed up were made. In the late 1960s and early 1970s, bobbing head dolls had round bases and a single wire face mask. Pairs of kissing dolls were made in the 1960s. There is a magnet inside the football player's cheek and the cheerleader has steel lips. They are about 3-1/2 inches to 4 inches tall. Kissing dolls were also made with the pair kissing lip to lip. They also made a rare "black face" doll during the late 1960s. A large store display doll, about 12 inches to 15 inches tall, was made in about 1962 and it is a prized collectible.

When purchasing a doll, check around the head for chips and cracks. Faded or chipped paint also detracts from a doll's price. Repainted and repaired dolls are not worth as much as original-condition dolls. Dolls in the original boxes are valued from 10% to 25% more, depending on the condition and graphics of the box.

New ceramic dolls, made as a collectible, are individually numbered and sometimes retail for as much as $50. This compares to the few dollars the originals sold for. Very few modern dolls will be played with or thrown away. Thus, it's not realistic to expect great leaps in price for these items down the road.

Doll	*Price Range*	
1961, square wood base, plain helmet, no "G" on helmet	50.00	125.00
1962-63, square ceramic base, "G" on helmet	35.00	100.00
1962-63, 12 inch, no base	250.00	650.00
1964-67, kissing dolls, lip to lip	50.00	175.00
1964-67, kissing dolls, lip to cheek	50.00	175.00
1965, round gold base, toes up	50.00	150.00

1967, round gold base, realistic face...50.00   150.00
1967, round gold base, black face...250.00   500.00
1967-73, round gold base, common variety.................................35.00   100.00
1970s, vinyl, round green base, toes up 25.00   75.00
1975, vinyl, buck teeth...20.00   45.00
1975, vinyl, smiling face, running 14.00   40.00
1996, ceramic, Brett Favre...50.00   75.00

1961 square wood base, plain helmet, no "G" on helmet ($50-$125).

1962-63 square ceramic base, "G" on helmet ($35-$100).

57

1963 square base, NFL embossed in gold on base ($50-$125).

1967-73, round gold base, common variety ($35-$100).

1965, round gold base, toes up ($50-$150).

1975, vinyl, smiling face, running, MIB ($25-$40).

1970s, vinyl, round green base, toes up ($25-$75).

Chapter 7

Books

The first book on the Packers was written in 1946 by Arch Ward. Chuck Johnson wrote another book about the Packers in 1961. Both of these early books were written about the Packers history. During the 1960s and 1970s, a lot of books were written by coaches and players from the championship teams of the 1960s. The success of the Holmgren era has sparked a resurgence in the number of modern books being written by coaches and players. Paperback books are usually worth less than hardcover books. Dust jackets

Lombardi on Football, **2 volumes, hard case, color photo on case ($50-$125).**

can add up to 25% to a book's price. Condition is very important when assessing a book's value. Missing pages, tears, stains and mildew all detract from a book's value. Check for autographs inside that can be worth more than the book itself.

Book	*Price Range*	
Bart Starr: A Biography, Bart Starr	20.00	45.00
Carroll Dale Scores Again, Harman (softcover)	10.00	30.00
Distant Replay, Jerry Kramer	15.00	35.00
Farewell to Football, Jerry Kramer	15.00	35.00
Football and the Single Man, Paul Hornung	20.00	45.00
Green Bay Packers, Arch Ward	25.00	75.00
Green Bay Packers, Chuck Johnson	20.00	45.00
Green Bay Packers, Pictorial Drama, Rainbolt	20.00	50.00
Instant Replay, Jerry Kramer	15.00	45.00
Lombardi, Jerry Kramer	20.00	45.00
Lombardi, Wiebush (great photo cover)	20.00	50.00
Lombardi: His Life and Times, Robert Wells	15.00	35.00
Lombardi on Football, 2 volumes, hard case, color photo on case	50.00	125.00
Lombardi on Football, 2 volumes, hard case, plain case	35.00	75.00

Lombardi on Football, 1 volume	25.00	60.00
Mean on Sunday, Ray Nitschke	25.00	55.00
My Life in Football, Bart Starr	10.00	25.00
One More July, (about Bill Curry), George Plimpton	20.00	45.00
Packer 75th Anniversary, limited signed edition	50.00	150.00
Packer 75th Anniversary, regular edition	30.00	65.00
Packer Legend, John Torinus (signed)	25.00	65.00
Packer Legend, John Torinus (unsigned)	15.00	40.00
Perspective on Victory, Bart Starr	20.00	45.00
Quarterbacking, Bart Starr	20.00	45.00
Run to Daylight, Vince Lombardi	25.00	55.00
Vince Lombardi, O'Brian	10.00	30.00
Vince Lombardi: Memories of a Special Time, Bynum	10.00	30.00

Football and the Single Man, **Paul Hornung ($20-$45).**

Green Bay Packers, **Chuck Johnson ($20-$45).**

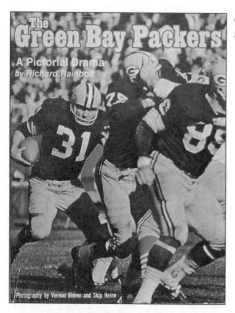

Green Bay Packers, Pictorial Drama, Richard Rainbolt ($20-$50).

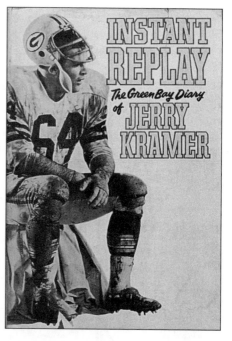

Instant Replay, Jerry Kramer ($15-$45).

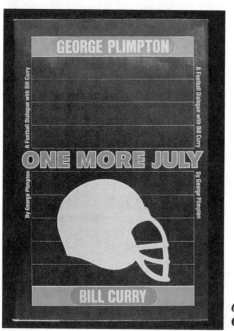

One More July, (about Bill Curry), George Plimpton ($20-$45).

Quarterbacking, **Bart Starr ($20-$45).**

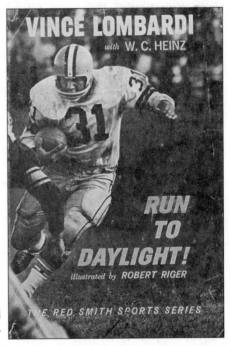

Run to Daylight, **Vince Lombardi ($25-$55).**

Single-Game Rushing Record

Dorsey Levens set the single-game rushing record with 190 yards in 33 carries against the Dallas Cowboys on Nov. 23, 1997. The Packers won the game, 45-17. This broke the old record of 186 yards that was set by Jim Taylor vs. the New York Giants on Dec. 3, 1961.

Chapter 8

Bottle Caps

Coca-Cola issued Packers players and All-Star players on the inside of its bottle caps from 1964-66 and a Packers set in 1971. In 1964, the bottle caps had no prefixes to their numbers. In 1965 and 1966, the caps had a C prefix. The 1971 set differs from the earlier sets in that the players photos were placed on the plastic cap liner, not printed on the caps themselves like the earlier sets. This set of bottle caps was placed on sheets and redeemed for prizes. Footballs, posters, pennants and other souvenirs could be traded for completed sheets. Condition of the caps is important when estimating their price. Caps that were never bent or used are the most valuable. Most caps came off bottles that were bent when removed. Rusty and severely dented caps have little value. The prices below are for caps in excellent condition.

1964-66 Coca-Cola Caps

Player	Price
Herb Adderley	5.00
Lionel Aldridge	2.00
Bill Anderson	2.00
Ken Bowman	2.00
Zeke Bratkowski	3.00
Tom Brown	2.00
Leroy Caffey	2.00
Don Chandler	2.00
Dennis Claridge	2.00
Tommy Joe Crutcher	2.00
Bill Curry	2.00
Carol Dale	2.00
Willie Davis	5.00
Boyd Dowler	2.00
Marv Flemming	2.00
Forrest Gregg	5.00
Hank Gremminger	2.00
Dan Grimm	2.00
Dave "Hog" Hanner	2.50

Doug Hart.. 2.00
Paul Hornung 8.00
Bob Jeter 2.00
Henry Jordan 5.00
Ron Kostelnik 2.00
Jerry Kramer 2.50
Bob Long.. 2.00
Max McGee.. 3.00
Rich Marshall... 2.00
Norm Masters... 2.00
Tom Moore 2.00
Ray Nitschke 7.00
Elijah Pitts 3.00
Dave Robinson... 2.00
Bob Skoronski.. 2.00
Ron Smith 2.00
Bart Starr 10.00
Jim Taylor 7.00
Fred "Fuzzy" Thurston... 2.50
Lloyd Voss 2.00
Willie Wood... 5.00
Steve Wright 2.00
Packer Logo 3.50

1971 Coca-Cola Green Bay Packers Caps

Player   *Price*

1. Ken Bowman.. 1.00
2. John Brockington 3.00
3. Bob Brown 1.50
4. Fred Carr 1.50
5. Jim Carter 1.00
6. Carroll Dale... 1.50
7. Ken Ellis.. 1.00
8. Gale Gillingham 1.50
9. Dave Hampton 1.50
10. Doug Hart.. 1.00
11. Jim Hill.. 1.00

12. Dick Himes 1.00

13. Scott Hunter 1.50

14. MacArthur Lane 2.50

15. Bill Lueck 1.00

16. Al Matthews 1.00

17. Rich McGeorge 1.00

18. Ray Nitschke 5.00

19. Francis Peay 1.00

20. Dave Robinson 1.00

21. Alden Roche 1.00

22. Bart Starr 10.00

Green Bay Packers Hall of Fame

More than 100 Packers players, coaches, trainers, presidents and other contributors have been inducted into the Green Bay Packers Hall of Fame:

1970: Bernard "Boob" Darling, Curly Lambeau, Lavvie Dilweg, Verne Lewellen, Jug Earp, Johnny "Blood" McNally, Cal Hubbard, Mike Michalske.

1972: Hank Bruder, Don Hutson, Milt Gantenbein, Cecil Isbell, Charles "Buckets" Goldenberg, Joe Laws, Arnie Herber, Russ Letlow, Clarke Hinkle, George Svendsen.

1973: Charlie Brock, Bobby Monnett, Tony Canadeo, Buford "Baby" Ray, Larry Craig, Andy Uram, Bob Forte, Dick Wildung, Ted Fritsch, H.L. "Whitey" Woodin.

1974: Al Carmichael, Dave Hanner, Fred Cone, Bill Howton, Bobby Dillon, John Martinkovic, Howie Ferguson, Jim Ringo, Bill Forester, Tobin Rote.

1975: Don Chandler, Ron Kramer, Willie Davis, Vince Lombardi, Paul Hornung, Max McGee, Henry Jordan, Jim Taylor, Jerry Kramer, Fred Thurston.

1976: Joseph "Red" Dunn, Bob Skoronski, Hank Gremminger, Jesse Whittenton, Gary Knafelc, Carl "Bud" Jorgensen.

1977: Howard "Cub" Buck, Bart Starr, Forrest Gregg, A.B. Turnbull, Charles Mathys Sr., Willie Wood.

1978: Boyd Dowler, Paul "Tiny" Engebretsen, Lon Evans, Ray Nitschke, George Calhoun.

1979: Nate Barrager, Carroll Dale, Elijah Pitts, Pete Tinsley, Dominic Olejniczak.

1981: Herb Adderley, Ken Bowman, Chester "Swede" Johnston, Lee H. Joannes.

1982: Lou Brock, Gale Gillingham, Dave Robinson, Jack Vainisi.

1983: Donny Anderson, Fred Carr, Carl Mulleneaux, Fred Leicht.

1984: John Brockington, Dan Currie, Eddie Jankowski, F.N. Trowbridge Sr.

1985: Phil Bengtson, Bob Jeter, Earl "Bud" Svendsen.

1986: Lee Roy Caffey, Irv Comp, Wilner Burke.

1987: Chester Marcol, Deral Teteak, Dr. E.S. Brusky.

1988: Lionel Aldridge, Bob Mann, Jerry Atkinson.

1989: Zeke Bratkowski, Ron Kostelnik.

1991: Harry Jacunski, Jan Stenerud, Gerald L. Clifford.

1992: Lynn Dickey, Larry McCarren, Al Schneider.

1993: Willie Buchanon, Johnnie Gray, Art Daley.

1994: Paul Coffman, Gerry Ellis, Dr. W. Webber Kelly.

1995: William Brault.

1996: John Anderson, Lee Remmel.

1997: John "Red" Cochran, Ezra Johnson, Travis Williams

Chapter 9

Buttons

Pinback buttons—for wear or display—are popular items. Many depict a team, player or a special event. Buttons range in size from more than 6 inches to less than an inch. Some larger buttons have both a pin to wear the button and a built-in stand to display it. Buttons from the 1930s to the 1950s are not easy to locate. Most pins were inexpensive or given away as premiums. Condition is important in determining value. Rust, stains, scratches, dents and fading all detract from a pin's price. Some buttons also had ribbons, footballs or helmets hanging from the bottom of the pin. Pins with just the Packers name or logo are less valuable than pins with player photos, team photos, special events or Championship and Super Bowl.

Years		*Regular*	*Championship*	
1920s (very rare)	45.00	150.00	n/a	
1930s (rare)	40.00	125.00	50.00	200.00
1940s	35.00	100.00	40.00	150.00
1950s	30.00	75.00	n/a	
1960s	15.00	45.00	30.00	75.00
1970s	10.00	25.00	n/a	
1980s	5.00	15.00	n/a	
1990s	2.00	10.00	3.00	15.00
1957 Stadium Dedication	20.00	50.00		
1972 "We Love Ray" (Nitschke)	10.00	35.00		

1969 Green Bay Packers Drenks Potato Chip Pins

Player	*Value Range*	
1. Herb Adderly	4.00	8.00
2. Lionel Aldridge	75	1.50
3. Donnie Anderson	1.50	3.00
4. Ken Bowman	50	1.00
5. Carroll Dale	75	1.50

6. Willie Davis 4.00   8.00

7. Boyd Dowler 1.50   3.00

8. Marv Fleming 1.50   3.00

9. Gale Gillingham..75   1.50

10. Jim Grabowski 1.50   3.00

11. Forrest Gregg 4.00   8.00

12. Don Horn...50   1.00

13. Bob Jeter 75   1.50

14. Henry Jordan 1.50   3.00

15. Ray Nitschke 5.00   10.00

16. Elijah Pitts 75   1.50

17. Dave Robinson 1.50   3.00

18. Bart Starr 8.00   16.00

19. Travis Williams..75   1.50

20. Willie Wood...4.00   8.00

1960 Championship with Division ribbons, green and gold ($25-$60).

1970s Packer Hall of Fame button with ribbon and metal football, 1-1/2" ($12-$30).

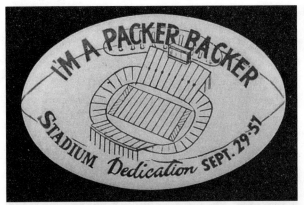

Stadium Dedication (Sept. 29, 1957), football shape, green and gold, 3" ($20-$50).

Buttons, from left—1980s "Gang Green; 1980s "Swat," both are green and gold ($7-$20 each).

1969 50-year button, football shape ($10-$20).

1960s Hotel Northland Packer Booster (Green Bay hotel), 1-1/4", round ($15-$30).

1960-61 Champion, gold with green lettering, b&w team photo in center, 3" ($35-$75).

1962 Hawg Hanner Day, 3" ($15-$30).

1967 booster, 1-1/4", premium from Heinz Foods ($10-$30).

1975-78 "74" Dave Roller Fan Club ($10-$20).

1971 "We Love Ray" (Nitschke), with ribbons, green and gold, football shape ($15-$40).

1980s "Mean Green," green and gold ($7-$20).

Chapter 10

Cigar Boxes

Cigar Boxes fall into two distinct categories. One is the plain "Green Bay Packer" box and the other is the "team photograph" box. The "Green Bay Packer" cigar box has only the wording; it's smaller and worth substantially less than the team photo box. The team photo cigar boxes are from the 1930s and 1940s. They are hard to find and command premium prices. The condition of the photograph and the year of team are both important factors in establishing a box's value. The Championship teams of 1936, 1939 and 1944 are the most pricey. The condition of the box and the photograph determine a box's value. A box with a severely damaged team photo is worth much less than one in good condition. The condition of the team photo is up to 75% of the box's value.

Year	*Price Range*	
1920s-1940s, plain with lettering only	20.00	50.00
1920s-1940s, all other team photo boxes not listed below	20.00	50.00
1929	75.00	250.00
1930	75.00	250.00
1931	75.00	250.00
1936, Championship team photo	50.00	200.00
1939, Championship team photo	50.00	200.00
1944, Championship team photo	50.00	200.00

Most Pass Receiving Yards in Game

1. Bill Howton vs. Los Angeles Rams, Oct. 21, 1956, 257 yards
2. Don Hutson vs. Brooklyn, Nov. 21, 1943, 237
3. Don Beebe vs. San Francisco, Oct. 14, 1996, 220
4. Don Hutson vs. Cleveland Rams, Oct. 18, 1942, 209
5. Don Hutson vs. Chicago Cardinals, Nov. 1, 1942, 207

Chapter 11

Decanters

There are three different Packers decanters made in the 1970s A #15 player in a throwing position that separates at the waist and has a cork stopper. A #87 player has a football in his arm and it also separates at the waist and has a cork stopper. The #15 decanter is almost 15 inches tall. The #87 decanter is about 12 inches tall. They were made in 1971. Neither has the Packers "G" on the helmet, indicating that they were not a licensed product. Both of these decanters are very popular. Another decanter is a #7 player with a football player in an unusual running pose. His helmet comes off and he has a cork stopper. He does have a round "G" on the helmet. This #7 decanter does not have the visual appeal that the #15 and

Liquor decanters, from left—#15 ($50-$95); #87 ($35-$75).

#87 decanter do. The #7 decanter is still collectible, but does not have as much value as the #15 and #87 decanters. Be careful with full decanters. The alcohol inside can eat away at the ceramic material and weaken the bottle. Be careful when handling these decanters—they can separate and fall! Also, be aware that there are laws in some states that restrict or prohibit the sale of bottles full of alcohol without a proper license.

No. on Decanter	*Price Range*	
15	50.00	95.00
87	35.00	75.00
7	25.00	60.00

Chapter 12

Envelopes and Stationary

Packers envelopes and stationary from the 1920s through 1940s are difficult to obtain. The 1950s and 1960s envelopes and stationary are easier to find and are a lot less valuable. Modern envelopes and stationary from the 1970s through the present are readily available and have minimal value. Look for colorful artwork that displays players, Championship years and special events. As with all paper items, look closely for stains, tears, holes, creases and fading that can detract from the price. Also, check any items for autographs that can increase the price.

Years	*Stationery*		*Envelopes*	
1920s (rare) 25.00	100.00		20.00	75.00
1930s 20.00	75.00		15.00	60.00
1940s 20.00	65.00		15.00	50.00
1950s 15.00	45.00		10.00	35.00
1960s 10.00	40.00		10.00	25.00
1970s 5.00	20.00		5.00	12.00
1980s 2.00	10.00		2.00	8.00
1990s 2.00	12.00		2.00	10.00

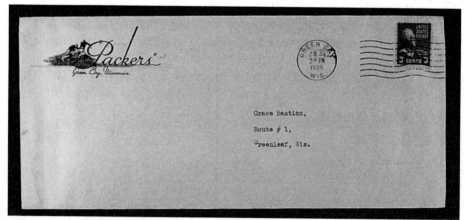

1939 Packer envelope ($30-$60).

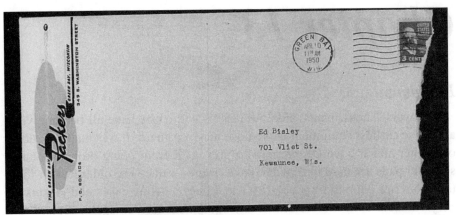

1950 Packer envelope, blue and gold ($15-$35).

1950s Packer stationary, blue and gold ($15-$35).

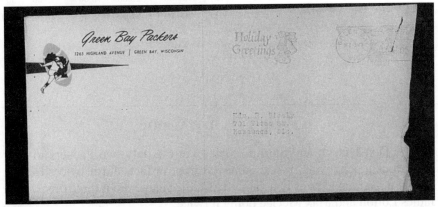

1963 Packer envelope, green and gold ($10-$25).

Chapter 13

Equipment

Players' shoes, pants, sideline jackets and capes have all become valuable. The earliest equipment is the nose mask or guard. It was made of rubber or leather and it covered the nose to prevent it from being broken. Leather shoulder pads are hard to find and have risen in value. The older leather high-top shoes are gaining in popularity and value. Sideline capes and jackets are very valuable collectibles. Check any equipment for damage or repairs. The modern players now wear gloves that are also desirable. Years ago, players used equipment as long as possible. Today, players have a large amount of equipment, making the modern items much easier to obtain. Any equipment from a Hall of Fame or star player is more valuable and should be priced at the higher end.

Years	Capes		Shoes		Jackets		Pants		Gloves	
1920s	-		100.00	300.00	-		100.00	450.00	-	
1930s	-		75.00	150.00	200.00	1,000.00	100.00	300.00	-	
1940s	-		60.00	125.00	150.00	750.00	75.00	200.00	-	
1950s	200.00	600.00	50.00	125.00	125.00	600.00	50.00	150.00	-	
1960s	200.00	600.00	50.00	125.00	100.00	500.00	50.00	150.00	-	
1970s	-		40.00	75.00	45.00	200.00	35.00	100.00	20.00	50.00
1980s	-		35.00	65.00	35.00	150.00	25.00	75.00	15.00	30.00
1990s	-		30.00	150.00	35.00	200.00	25.00	125.00	10.00	50.00

Four TDs in a Game

Don Hutson and Sterling Shape are the only two Packers to ever catch four touchdowns in one game. Sharpe, in fact, did it twice. Hutson caught three touchdowns in a game six times; Sharpe did it three times, with James Lofton and Max McGee doing it twice.

Chapter 14

Games

The two most popular Packers board games are the Bart Starr game and the Vince Lombardi game. The Bart Starr game is from 1968. It is oversized with a large number of cards and an illustration of Bart Starr in the box. The Vince Lombardi game has two editions. The 1970 edition has a large color picture of Lombardi on the cover. The 1973 edition is less common, but also has a much smaller picture of Lombardi on the cover. Lombardi's color picture makes his game very popular with Packers collectors. Jerry Kramer's football game (Instant Replay) from 1970, is also popular with collectors. Some of the Electric football games also show Packers on the cover or had players that could be made into Packers. Because of the illustrations on the front of the box, as much as 75% of a game's value is determined by the condition of the box. Also, check to see if all the pieces are there. Incomplete games are not worth as much as complete ones.

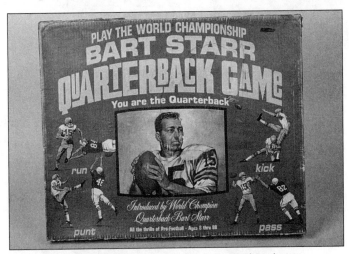

Bart Starr Quarterback Game, oversized ($25-$100).

Game	*Price Range*	
Bart Starr Quarterback Game, oversized 25.00	100.00+
Jerry Kramer Instant Replay 15.00	45.00

NFL Electric Football, Tudor, Model #510, Packer/Colts......................30.00   95.00

NFL Electric Football-Tudor, Model #619, Packer/Lions......................15.00   45.00

Official NFL Football Game, Packer/49ers 20.00   45.00

Vince Lombardi's Game, great Lombardi photo on cover 25.00   75.00

Official NFL All-Pro Football Game (Packers/49ers), 1967 ($20-$45).

Vince Lombardi's Game, 1970 ($25-$75).

Chapter 15

Glasses, Cups and Mugs

Glasses, cups and mugs are excellent items to collect. They can be both used and displayed. Glasses form the 1930s to the 1950s are difficult to find. Two of the more popular early glasses are the "Don Hutson's Playdium" glasses and the "Miller" beer glasses of the late 1940s and early 1950s. The "Playdium" glasses came in a large tumbler size and a small juice size. They depicted a color cartoon character of two football players. They are hard to find and command premium prices. The "Miller High Life" glass is small but very colorful. It has "Packer Backer" printed on it with a green football player on a gold background. It was produced for the Burr Distributing Co., and was only available in Northeast Wisconsin.

The success of the 1960s teams spawned a lot of glasses from the 1960s and 1970s. The "Pizza Hut" glass from the early 1970s are very popular. They have a large "head shot" of five players and coach Lombardi. The photos are very clear and information about each is printed on the back of the glass. Lombardi, Starr, Nitschke, Hornung, Davis and Kramer are pictured on the glass. Because five of the six are in the Hall of Fame (and, Kramer, the sixth, should be!) this set has excellent potential for future value. The Pizza Hut glasses were only available in Wisconsin. Make sure to check for cracks and chips.

Cups (7-Eleven)

Year/Player	Price Range	
1972 Gale Gillingham	2.00	4.00
1973 John Brockington	2.00	4.00
1973 Scott Hunter	2.00	4.00
1973 Mike McCoy	2.00	4.00

Glasses

Years	Price Range	
1930s	50.00	100.00
1940s Miller glass with player	25.00	45.00
1940s Playdium Large	50.00	100.00

1940s Playdium Small	35.00	75.00
1950s	25.00	75.00
1960s Championship	15.00	45.00
1970s Pizza Hut, Lombardi or Starr, each	40.00	45.00
1970s Pizza Hut, Nitschke, Hornung, Davis, Kramer	20.00	25.00
1980s	3.00	15.00
1990s	3.00	15.00

Mugs

### Years	### Price Range	
Pre-1960	35.00	100.00
1960s newspaper headlines	25.00	75.00
1960s coffee mug, Packers logo	15.00	45.00
1970s coffee mug, Packers logo	10.00	30.00
1980s coffee mug, Packers logo	5.00	15.00
1990s coffee mug, Packers logo	5.00	15.00

Steins, from left—75th Anniversary ($30-$75); limited edition, Lombardi ($75-$100+); 1960s, helmet logo, Japan ($50-$95).

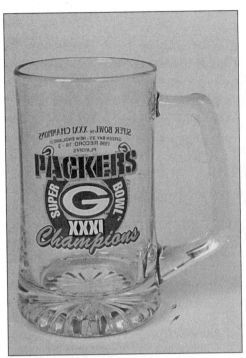

1997 Super Bowl XXXI, glass mug ($4-$10).

1940s Miller glass with player ($25-$45).

Mugs, from left—1965 Championship, newspaper sports page ($45-$65); 1967 Super Bowl I, newspaper sports page ($50-$75).

1970s Pizza Hut glasses, from left—Starr ($45); Lombardi ($45); Hornung ($25); Nitschke ($25); Kramer ($20); Davis ($25).

Glasses, from left—1962 "NFL World Champions," with pennants on opposite side ($20-$40); 1964, signatures of players and coaches, green and gold ($20-$40).

Glasses, from left—1967, Mobile Oil premium, gold shield ($10-$20); 1968, Mobile Oil premium, gold shield ($10-$20).

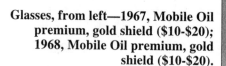

Chapter 16

Helmets

The early Packers leather helmets from the 1920s are nearly impossible to find. Many of the early 1920s players wore no helmets at all! In the 1930s and 1940s, a large variety of leather helmets were used. Some were stamped "Packers" on the front panel, while other helmets need documentation to verify that they were worn by a Packers player. In the early 1950s, plastic helmets replaced leather ones. the face-bar did not become widely used until the late 1950s. Any Packers helmet that has a "G" on it is 1961 or newer. The 1960s helmets had web suspension that was replaced in the 1970s with both liquid and air chambers that covered the inside of the helmet.

One of the main factors in estimating a helmet's value is the player who wore it. Hall of Fame players can be worth five to 10 times the price of a regular player's helmet. Condition is also important in determining price. Leather helmets were sometimes repaired and repainted. Plastic helmets should be checked for cracks and repairs. Modern helmets—identical to the players' helmets—are now being sold in stores. This is making it difficult to distinguish between a souvenir helmet and an actual player helmet. Always try to find as much information about a helmet as possible. Helmets are very popular items to have autographed. If you obtain a signed helmet, put it in a case to preserve the signatures.

Years	_Price Range_	
1920s (rare)	500.00	2,000.00+
1930s	400.00	1,500.00+
1940s	350.00	1,500.00+
1950s	250.00	1,250.00+
1960s	250.00	1,250.00+
1970s	200.00	600.00+
1980s	150.00	500.00+
1990s	150.00	450.00+

Chapter 17

Jerseys

1920s Packers jerseys are about impossible to find. Numbers were not placed on jerseys until 1929. This makes it very difficult to determine if a jersey was worn by a player. The 1920s jerseys were made out of a thick heavy sweater-like material. In the 1930s, jerseys were made out of a lighter knit material. Knit material was used for jerseys until about 1970 when mesh jerseys were used. They have small holes and are made out of a much lighter material. Up until the 1990s, jerseys were used more than one season. Jerseys from Championship and Super Bowl years are worth more. Jerseys that were worn by Hall of Fame players can be worth up to 10 times the value of regular players. Names were not placed on the back of jerseys until the early 1970s. Companies now make souvenir jerseys identical to the player jerseys. Obtain jerseys directly from the team or player when possible. Documentation for a jersey's age and origin will increase its value. Holes, tears, stains and major repairs can detract from a jersey's value.

Years	_Price Range_	
1920s (rare)	1,000.00	5,000.00+
1930s	750.00	4,000.00+
1940s	500.00	3,500.00+
1950s	400.00	3,000.00+
1960s	350.00	2,500.00+
1970s	250.00	1,000.00+
1980s	100.00	500.00+
1990s	100.00	500.00+

Here are some specific examples of the value of jerseys:

Year/Player	_Price_
1960s Ray Nitschke, home, game worn	2,450.00
1960s Bart Starr, home, game worn, autographed	3,750.00
1980s Lynn Dickey, white, game worn	500.00
1980s Estus Hood, white, mesh, game worn	125.00
1980s James Lofton, home, game worn	700.00

1990s Tony Mandarich, home, game worn..475.00
1990s Reggie White, white, game worn 1,400.00
1993 LeRoy Butler, home, game worn, autographed 500.00
1993 Mark Clayton, home, game worn..575.00
1993 Brett Favre, home, game worn..1,250.00
1993 Sterling Sharpe, white, game worn, autographed 1,250.00
1994 Brett Favre, throwback, 75th Anniversary patch, game worn 900.00

Late-1970s away jersey, team issue ($75-$150).

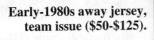

Early-1980s away jersey, team issue ($50-$125).

Early-1990s away jersey, team issue ($50-$125).

Chapter 18

Jewelry

The most valuable jewelry items are the Super Bowl I, II and XXXI Packers rings. These highly sought rings can range in value from a few thousand for a sample ring, to more than $30,000 for a Hall of Fame player's ring. Rings, cufflinks, tie bars, tie tacks and watches are all treasured collectibles. Jewelry that was given to players and coaches is very desirable and commands high prices. Souvenir jewelry sold at retail stores during the 1950s through the 1970s is also becoming very collectible. Estimating the age of jewelry can be difficult. Any jewelry with the Packers "G" is from the 1960s or newer. When purchasing jewelry, check for damage or repairs, chips, cracks and scratches. Solid

Belt buckle, 1960s, football shape ($10-$30).

gold is usually marked 10K, 12K or 14K. Gold-filled jewelry will have the initials "G.F." or be marked "gold filled." The majority of the gold- and silver-colored jewelry is plated. Unless marked sterling, most silver-colored jewelry is not solid silver.

Years	*Real Item*		*Sample Item*	
Super Bowl I ring 6,000.00	25,000.00		2,000.00	4,000.00
Super Bowl II ring 6,000.00	25,000.00		2,000.00	4,000.00
Super Bowl XXXI ring 5,000.00	20,000.00		2,000.00	4,000.00
1965 Championship ring 5,000.00	15,000.00		2,000.00	3,500.00
1962 Championship watch 1,000.00	3,500.00		n/a	
1961 Championship ring 4,500.00	15,000.00		2,000.00	3,500.00
1944 Championship watch 1,000.00	5,000.00		n/a	

Belt buckle, 1978, helmet, brass finish ($10-$30).

Belt buckle, 1978, Large "G" ($8-$20).

Belt buckle, Super Bowl XXXI, pewter ($10-$25).

1970s key ring, plastic, red football ($5-$15).

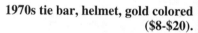

Late-1960s/early-1970s key ring, leather with metal fob ($10-$25).

1970s tie bar, helmet, gold colored ($8-$20).

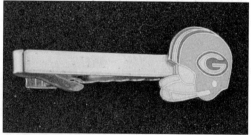

Dan Devine key ring, metal, team issued ($10-$30).

1960s/1970s tie bar, silver colored
($10-$25).

75th Anniversary key ring, plastic
($4-$8).

1960s cufflinks, gold colored ($10-$25).

1960s key chain, plastic, shield shape
($10-$25).

1969 "50 Years" tie bar ($25-$35).

Tie bar ($20-$30).

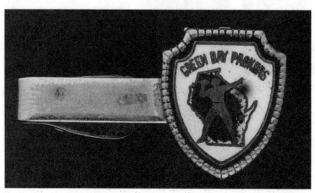

Tie bar ($20-$30).

Chapter 19

Lamps

Packers helmet lamps make both an excellent collectible and a practical item for the home. Beginning in the 1960s, helmet lamps were available in both hanging and table models. The small plastic hel-

met lamp dated 1973 makes an excellent bedroom or children's lamp. Full-sized official "Riddell" helmet lamps can be very costly. Souvenir helmet lamps can be much less expensive and just as attractive. Hanging full-

1960s full-size Riddel helmet with wood base ($100-$300).

sized helmet lamps from the 1960s and 1970s are difficult to find and are increasing in value. Getting helmet lamps autographed can increase their price.

1973 helmet lamp, 6" ($20-$45).

Year	*PriceRange*	
1930s (very rare)	100.00	500.00
1940s	75.00	350.00
1950s	50.00	250.00
1960s helmet lamp (hanging)	75.00	250.00
1960s helmet lamp (table)	100.00	325.00
1970s helmet lamp (hanging)	50.00	150.00
1970s helmet lamp (table)	75.00	250.00
1973 small helmet lamp	20.00	50.00
1980s helmet lamp (all kinds)	75.00	250.00
1990s helmet lamp (all kinds)	75.00	250.00

Chapter 20

Magazines

Currently, the most popular magazine to collect is *Sports Illustrated. SI* started in 1954 and continues today. Many 1960s Hall of Famers and current players are on the covers. Many other magazines had Packers on the cover, including *The Sporting News, Sport, Pro Football weekly* and *Street & Smith*. Getting the cover autographed by the player or players on the cover can increase the value significantly. Always check magazines to make sure they are complete and the cover isn't loose. Tears, stains, creases, cut pictures, mildew and writing all decrease a magazine's value. Store them in an acid-free plastic bag or paper envelope. Keep them in a clean, dry area. When a magazine is framed or displayed, avoid direct sunlight and bright lighting that will cause fading. Curly Lambeau, Don Hutson, Vince Lombardi, Bart Starr, Mike Holmgren, Brett Favre, Reggie White and many others have been featured on many magazines covers.

Date	*Cover Subject*	*Price Range*	

All Pro Football (annual)

1963	Bart Starr	10.00	30.00
1967	Carroll Dale	5.00	15.00

Dell's-Pro Football Review (annual)

1961	Paul Hornung	15.00	50.00
1962	Jim Taylor	15.00	50.00
1967	Bart Starr	15.00	45.00
1968	Donny Anderson	10.00	30.00

Fawcett's-Pro Football (annual)

1961	Paul Hornung	10.00	30.00
1962	Jim Taylor	8.00	25.00
1963	Jim Taylor	7.00	20.00

Football Digest

4/68	Bart Starr	10.00	30.00
3/72	John Brockington	4.00	10.00

3/73	John Brockington	5.00	15.00
12/83	Lynn Dickey	2.00	6.00
11/86	James Lofton	3.00	8.00

Inside Football-Sport Magazine (annual)

1962	Jim Taylor 10.00	25.00	
1969	Vince Lombardi (Redskins) 5.00	15.00	

NFL Yearbook

1967	Donny Anderson	10.00	30.00

Pro Football Annual (Sport Magazine)

1967	Bart Starr	10.00	30.00

Pro Football Illustrated (annual)

1962	Paul Hornung	10.00	30.00

Pro Football Stars (annual)

1962	Bart Starr	15.00	40.00
1963	Jim Taylor	12.00	35.00
1964	Paul Hornung	10.00	30.00

Pro Football Weekly

10/5/67	Bart Starr	10.00	30.00
11/17/67	Bart Starr	8.00	20.00
10/12/67	Packers/Cowboys	8.00	20.00
12/7/67	Lombardi/Starr	10.00	25.00

Sport

11/56	Paul Hornung (Notre Dame)	8.00	20.00
11/61	Paul Hornung	7.00	15.00
1/63	Paul Hornung	5.00	12.00
1/64	Jim Taylor	6.00	15.00
4/66	Paul Hornung	7.00	15.00
12/67	Bart Starr	7.00	20.00
7/70	Bart Starr	6.00	15.00

The Sporting News

12/4/65	Anderson/Grabowski	5.00	15.00
1/15/66	Vince Lombardi	10.00	25.00
1/7/67	Bart Starr	8.00	20.00
12/16/67	Vince Lombardi	8.00	20.00
1/6/68	Green Bay Packers	6.00	18.00
1/13/68	Lombardi/Starr	10.00	25.00
1/27/68	Donny Anderson	5.00	15.00
11/23/68	Bart Starr	8.00	20.00
1/1/72	Jerry Tagge	4.00	10.00
11/4/91	Ty Detmer	2.00	6.00
10/19/92	Don Majkowski	2.00	5.00
7/12/93	Reggie White	5.00	12.00

The Sporting News Football Register (annual)

1969	Bart Starr	15.00	40.00

Sports All-Stars (annual)

1963	Jim Taylor	10.00	25.00

Sports Illustrated

10/29/56	Paul Hornung (Notre Dame)	15.00	40.00
11/12/56	Ron Kramer (Michigan)	6.00	12.00
9/25/61	Bart Starr	15.00	35.00
12/1/61	Dan Currie	8.00	20.00
9/10/62	Jim Taylor	10.00	30.00
5/20/63	Paul Hornung	10.00	30.00
1/10/66	Jim Taylor	10.00	30.00
10/31/66	Bart Starr	15.00	35.00
1/9/67	Bart Starr	15.00	40.00
1/23/67	Max McGee (Super Bowl I)	20.00	50.00
8/14/67	Jim Taylor (Saints)	8.00	20.00
1/8/68	Chuck Mercein (Ice Bowl)	8.00	25.00
1/22/68	Vince Lombardi (Super Bowl II)	20.00	50.00
7/15/68	Ray Nitschke	8.00	25.00
12/16/68	Colts vs. Packers	5.00	15.00

3/3/69	Vince Lombardi (Redskins)	8.00	20.00
7/28/69	Vince Lombardi (Redskins)	8.00	20.00
8/25/75	Bart Starr	8.00	20.00
9/28/92	Tony Mandarich	2.00	5.00

Sports Review (annual)
| 1967 | Bart Starr | 10.00 | 25.00 |

Sports Stars of Pro Football (annual)
| 1968 | Bart Starr | 10.00 | 25.00 |

Street & Smith's Pro Football (annual)
| 1964 | Bart Starr | 25.00 | 60.00 |

True Football Yearbook
| 1963 | Herb Adderly | 10.00 | 25.00 |
| 1967 | Bart Starr | 10.00 | 25.00 |

Jan. 10, 1966, Sports Illustrated, Jim Taylor ($10-$30).

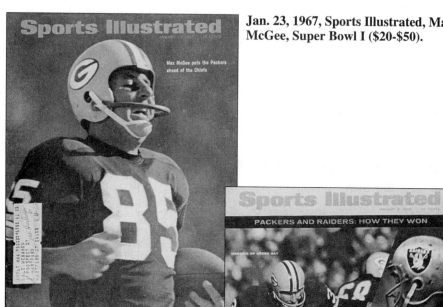

Jan. 23, 1967, Sports Illustrated, Max McGee, Super Bowl I ($20-$50).

Jan. 8, 1968, Sports Illustrated, Chuck Mercein, Ice Bowl ($8-$25).

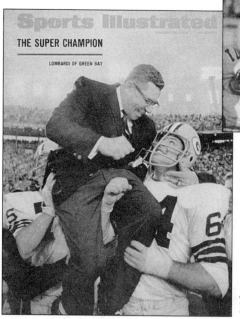

Jan. 22, 1969, Sports Illustrated, Vince Lombardi, Super Bowl II ($20-$50).

1960s Packers signed football

1996 Upper Deck, #131

1996 Topps Stadium Club, #60

1995 Flair, #76

1995 Flair, #78

1970s pennant

1994 GameDay, #147

1994 GameDay, #149

1960s round-base
bobbing head

1990s team-signed helmet

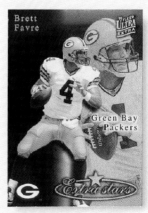

1996 Pro Line III, #99   **1995 Score Summit, #32**   **1995 Fleer Ultra, #490**

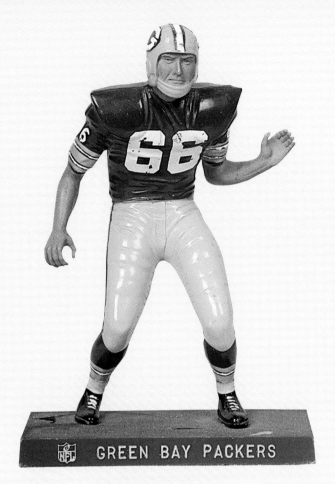

1960s Hartland statue

**1995 Score Summit
Backfield Stars, #15**

1997 Pacific, #54

1995 Fleer Ultra, #433

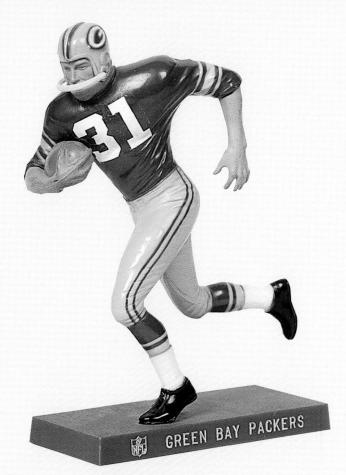

1960s Hartland statue

1995 Fleer Metal, #48

1996 Pro Line, #62

Packers Mr. Boston bottle, #15

1996 SkyBox, #62

1995 Fleer Ultra, #111

1995 Prime Playoff, #172

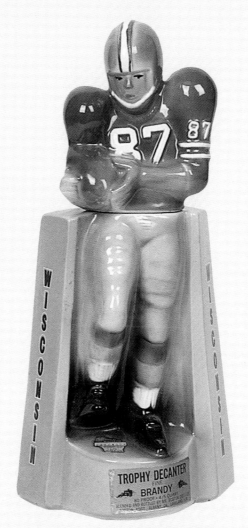

Packers Mr. Boston bottle, #87

1996 Pinnacle, #98

1995 Stadium Club, #114

1964 Packers glass **1962 Championship glass**

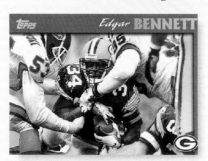

1997 Topps, #356

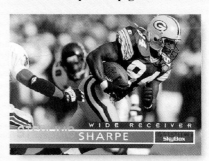

1995 SkyBox Impact, #55

1996 SkyBox, #240

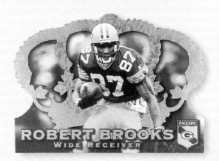

1996 Pacific, #CR-115

Chapter 21

Miscellaneous

There are many unique and unusual Packers items. Pens, pencils, nigh-lights, mirrors, tables, chairs, garbage cans, clothing, key chains, bike reflectors, stand-up cardboard cutouts and many novelty and one-of-a-kind items. Prices vary according to the item's visual appeal, functionality, rarity and general demand. As with all collectibles, condition is a factor in evaluating an item's price. Use common sense when pricing or evaluating value. Here are a few miscellaneous items to look for:

RC Cola cans: In 1976-77, Royal Crown Cola issued several Packers players on its soda cans (as well as for several other teams). Cans that were opened on the bottom are the most valuable.

Trays: Trays are interesting and provide a unique collectible that make for excellent display. The earliest is a small metal rectangular tray with a 1931 Championship team photograph in the center. It was made to advertise "Pale Ale" and is quite valuable. Most trays before the 1960s are metal. During the 1960s to the present, both metal and plastic were used. The condition of the tray is an important factor in assessing its value. Watch out for scratches, stains, chips, dents and fading. Team photographs, player photographs and stadium photographs all add to the price. Any tray with the Packers "G" on it is from the 1960s or newer.

RC Cola cans

Player	Price Range	
John Brockington	5.00	8.00
Fred Carr	4.00	6.00
Lynn Dickey	5.00	8.00
Bob Hyland	3.00	5.00
Chester Marcol	3.00	5.00
Mike McCoy	3.00	5.00
Rich McGeorge	3.00	5.00
Steve Odom	3.00	5.00
Clarence Williams	3.00	5.00

Trays

Year		Price Range
1930s	100.00	300.00
1940s	75.00	250.00
1950s	50.00	100.00
1960s	35.00	100.00
1970s	15.00	35.00
1980s	10.00	30.00
1990s	5.00	25.00

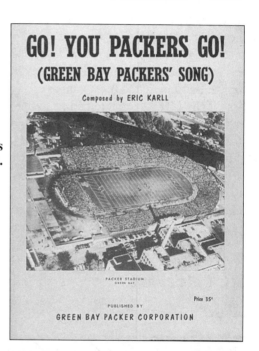

Sheet music, 1950, "Go! You Packers Go!", stadium photo ($25-$50).

1960s Packers pen with viewing window ($15-$35).

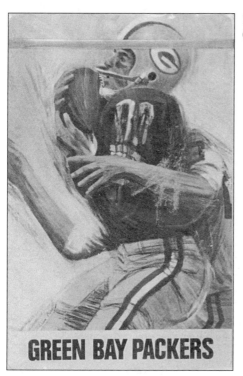

1960s playing cards, unopened ($10-$30).

1930s/40s wall hanging, 5 feet tall, plaster and horse hair, steel rod, very rare display piece that hung in the Packers office ($1,000-$3,000).

1970s ice bucket, green and gold, with stadium, championship years and coaches ($35-$75).

1960s bike reflector, red plastic, 3" ($10-$20).

1960s breast patch, three mounting pins on back, metallic thread, team issue ($50-$95).

1993, 75th Anniversary patch ($15-$40).

1978 clothes brush ($5-$15).

1970s night light, plastic with helmet logo ($8-$15).

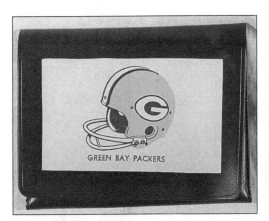

1970s credit card holder, schedule inside, plastic, green ($8-$20).

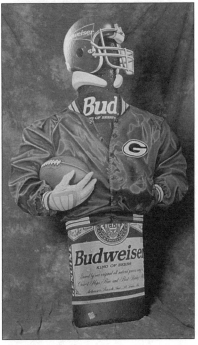

Cardboard cutout, Bud bottle with Packers coat ($25-$45).

1996 Packer Backer patch, 3" ($5-$12).

Cardboard cutout, life-size, Brett Favre, Mountain Dew ($50-$95).

Cardboard cutout, life-size, Mike Holmgren ($50-$95).

Cardboard cutout, life-size, Reggie White, Ford dealer promotion ($60-$125).

Chapter 22

Newspapers

Packers newspapers from the 1920s are pricey and not easy to find. Newspapers from Championship and Super Bowl games are the most valuable. Newspapers make an excellent item to frame. Newspapers brown with age, making white copies difficult to locate. Tears, holes, creases, stains and mildew all detract from a paper's value. Newspapers are susceptible to damage, making condition very important in assessing value.

The three grades of newspapers are Excellent, Good-Very Good and Poor-Fair. Excellent condition will be nearly new looking with little yellowing and only light creasing. Good-Very Good condition may have some yellowing, minor creasing, very light stains and small tears. The overall appearance should be nice. Poor-Fair condition will have major damage such as holes, severe staining, large rips and an almost brown color. Poor-Fair condition newspapers have little value.

Years	*Regular Game*		*Championship Game*	
1920s (rare)	25.00	75.00+	n/a	
1930s	15.00	35.00	20.00	50.00+
1940s	10.00	30.00	15.00	45.00+
1950s	8.00	25.00	n/a	
1960s	6.00	20.00	15.00	45.00
1970s	3.00	10.00	n/a	
1980s	3.00	10.00	n/a	
1990s	2.00	5.00	3.00	10.00
1957, Stadium Dedication	10.00	25.00		
1965, Lambeau Dies	8.00	20.00		
1970, Lombardi Dies	10.00	25.00		

Super Bowl MVPs

Bart Starr was the MVP of Super Bowls I and II. Desmond Howard took the honors in the 1996 Super Bowl

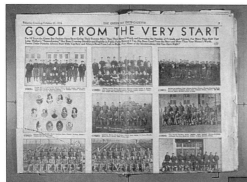

Oct. 27, 1934, Green Bay Press-Gazette, Packers team photos ($15-$40).

Nov. 9, 1935, Green Bay Press-Gazette, Packers team photo and articles ($8-$25).

1945 sports section, Green Bay Press-Gazette with Don Hutson photo ($5-$20).

Sept. 30, 1957, front section, Green Bay Press-Gazette, Stadium Dedication ($20-$45).

Dec. 18, 1960, single-page extra, Green Bay Press-Gazette, Packers beat Rams to cinch Western Conference ($8-$25).

Jan 1, 1962, single-page extra, Green Bay Press-Gazette, Packers win 1961 Championship ($30-$60).

Jan 1, 1962, Milwaukee Sentinel, Packers win 1961 championship ($25-$50).

1960, sports section, Green Bay Press-Gazette, Lombardi Coach of the Year ($15-$35).

1960s, sports section, Green Bay Press-Gazette, Lombardi articles ($8-$20).

June 2, 1965, sports section, Green Bay Press-Gazette, Curly Lambeau dies ($8-$20).

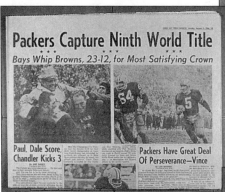

Jan. 3, 1966, sports section, Green Bay Press-Gazette, Packers win 1965 Championship ($20-$50).

Jan. 16, 1967, front page, Green Bay Press-Gazette, Packers win Super Bowl I ($30-$60).

Jan. 16, 1967, sports section, Green Bay Press-Gazette, Packers win Super Bowl I ($30-$60).

Jan. 2, 1968, front page, Green Bay Press-Gazette, Packers win 1966 Championship, Ice Bowl ($25-$50).

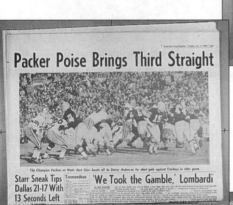

Jan. 2, 1968, sports section, Green Bay Press-Gazette, Packers win 1966 Championship, Ice Bowl ($30-$60).

Jan. 15, 1968, sports section, Green Bay Press-Gazette, Packers win Super Bowl II ($20-$50).

Jan. 15, 1968, sports section, The Miami Herald, Packers win Super Bowl II ($15-$30).

Sept. 21, 1969, 50-year history of the Packers, four sections of Green Bay Press-Gazette ($15-$40).

Sept. 21, 1969, section of 50-year history of the Packers, Green Bay Press-Gazette.

Sept. 21, 1969, section of 50-year history of the Packers, Green Bay Press-Gazette.

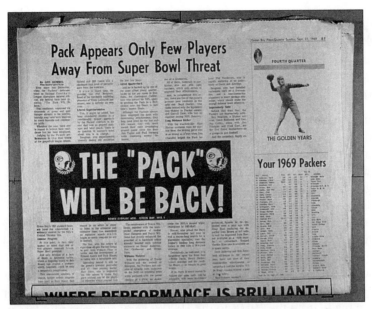

Sept. 21, 1969, section of 50-year history of the Packers, Green Bay Press-Gazette.

Dec. 12, 1971, sports section, Green Bay Press- Gazette, Ray Nitschke Day ($10-$30).

Chapter 23

Pennants

Pennants are popular due to their attractiveness and displayability. Pennants from the 1920s and 1930s are very rare and command premium prices. Early pennants were made from felt and many had sewn-on lettering. Championship and Super Bowl pennants are the most valuable. Determining a pennant's age can be difficult. Many pennants were not dated. Any pennants with a helmet displaying the Packers "G" is 1961 or newer.

Photo pennants from the 1960s are very collectible. They have a square cutout on the left side of the pennant. A picture of a player or team was glued or taped from the back side of the pennant. The condition of the photograph is important to determine price. If the photo is missing, the pennant has little value. About 50% of a pennant's value is in the condition the photo. Smaller mini-pennants were made from the 1950s to the 1990s. They are generally less valuable than a full-sized pennant of the same age and design.

Keep pennants in a plastic sleeve or have them framed, if possible. Condition is important because most pennants were hung on walls with tacks or nails. Stains, holes, cracking, fading and missing tips all detract from a pennant's price. The three conditions of pennants are Poor-Fair, Good-Very Good and Excellent. Poor-Fair pennants will have major damage such as holes, missing tips, tears, cracks, stains and fading. Good-Very Good condition pennants can have only small pin hole and very light cracking, staining or fading. Excellent condition pennants will be almost new, without any defects that are easily noticed.

Years	*Regular Pennant*		*Championship Pennant*	
1920s (very rare)	75.00	200.00+	n/a	
1930s (rare)	50.00	125.00	100.00	300.00
1940s	50.00	125.00	75.00	250.00
1950s	40.00	100.00	n/a	
1960s	20.00	75.00	50.00	200.00
1960s team or player photo pennants	45.00	125.00	n/a	
1970s	10.00	45.00	n/a	
1980s	5.00	30.00	n/a	
1990s	2.00	10.00	3.00	10.00

1960s, green and gold, runner with state and football in background ($50-$100).

1960s, green and gold, passer with state in background ($45-$95).

1960s, Championship, #15 passing ($60-$150).

Late 1960s/early 1970s, helmet with single-bar face mask, c1967 ($25-$50).

Late 1970s, helmet with double-bar face mask ($15-$35).

Late 1970s, helmet with double-bar face mask, very colorful ($15-$35).

1980s, helmet with newer face mask $10-$20).

No Interceptions, Please

Did you know that Bart Starr holds the Packers record for most passes thrown without an interception? He wasn't picked off in 294 attempts from 1964-65.

Chapter 24

Phone Cards

A relatively new collecting area is pre-paid phone cards. Several Packers cards have been made and are quite popular.

Card	_No. Made_	_Date Made_	_Price_
ACMI Packer Hall of Fame Willie Davis $3 card 2,500		3-94	10.00
ACMI Packer Hall of Fame Willie Davis $7 card 1,500		3-94	12.00
ACMI Packer Hall of Fame Vince Lombardi $3 card 2,500		3-94	10.00
ACMI Packer Hall of Fame Vince Lombardi $7 card 1,500		3-94	12.00
ACMI Packer Hall of Fame Lombardi/Starr $3 card 2,500		11-94	10.00
ACMI Packer Hall of Fame Lombardi/Starr $7 card 1,500		11-94	12.00
ACMI Packer Hall of Fame Ray Nitschke $3 card 2,500		3-94	10.00
ACMI Packer Hall of Fame Ray Nitschke $7 card 2,500		3-94	12.00
ACMI Packer Hall of Fame Ray Nitschke $20 card 700		3-94	25.00
ACMI Packer Hall of Fame Bart Starr $3 card 2,500		3-94	10.00
ACMI Packer Hall of Fame Bart Starr $7 card 2,500		3-94	12.00
Amerivox Bart Starr $10 card... 2,000		11-93	25.00

Chapter 25

Photographs

Photographs of the 1920s are difficult to find. Most early photographs were taken by Otto Stiller. He was the Packers official photographer. Championship team photos from 1929, 1930, 1931, 1936, 1939, 1944, 1961, 1962, 1965, 1966, 1967 and 1996 are more valuable than non-championship team photographs. Stadium and game-action photos are always at a premium. Photographs range in size from a few inches to 6 feet long. The majority of 1920s to 1960s photographs are black and white. Press photos are usually 8-inch by 10-inch black-and-white photos with a stamp on the back from the photographer, newspaper or wire service.

1956 Bart Starr photo, b&w, 8" x 10", rare first-year signature, personalized to Packers player: signed ($150-$500); unsigned ($35-$75).

When purchasing photographs, check for fading, holes, cracks, stains, tears and writing that detract from a photograph's value. Autographs can increase the value of a photo. Photos fall into two categories for pricing: Excellent condition (almost new with only very minor wear), and Good condition (minor wear but no severe damage that would detract from its visual appeal). Photographs that are heavily damaged have minimal value. The prices listed are for original photographs, not recent copies. Photocopies or new photos made from old negatives are not as valuable as original old photos.

Years	*Player Photos*		*Team Photos*		*Stadium Photos*		*Game Action Photos*	
1920s (rare)	25.00	75.00	50.00	200.00	50.00	200.00	45.00	150.00
1930s	20.00	60.00	40.00	150.00	45.00	150.00	40.00	125.00
1940s	15.00	40.00	35.00	125.00	30.00	125.00	25.00	100.00
1950s	10.00	30.00	25.00	75.00	25.00	100.00	20.00	75.00
1960s	5.00	25.00	15.00	50.00	20.00	75.00	20.00	65.00
1970s	3.00	12.00	10.00	30.00	15.00	50.00	15.00	35.00
1980s	3.00	10.00	5.00	20.00	10.00	30.00	10.00	35.00
1990s	2.00	10.00	3.00	15.00	5.00	25.00	5.00	15.00

1917 team photo, b&w, 8" x 10", Stiller ($30-$50).

1918 team photo, b&w, 8" x 10", Stiller ($30-$50).

1919 team photo, b&w, 8" x 10", Stiller ($30-$50).

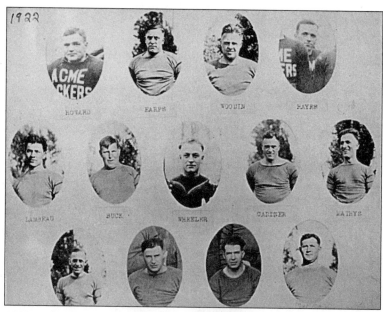

1922 team photo, b&w, 8" x 10", Stiller ($35-$55).

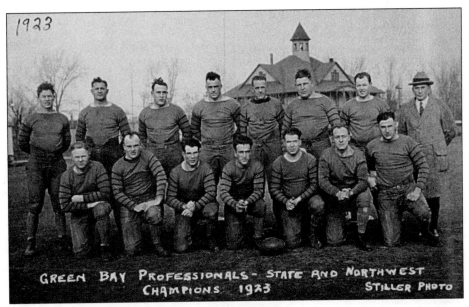

1923 team photo, b&w, 8'' x 10'', Stiller ($40-$55).

1924 team photo, b&w, 8'' x 10'', Stiller ($40-$55).

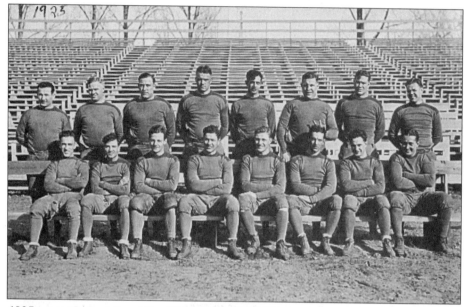

1925 team photo, b&w, 8" x 10", Stiller ($40-$55).

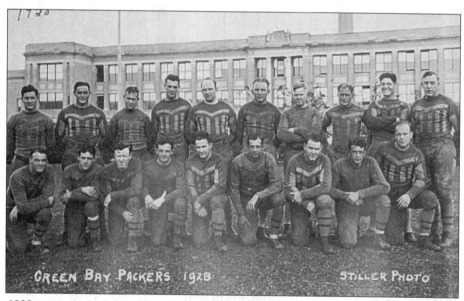

1928 team photo, b&w, 8" x 10", Stiller ($40-$55).

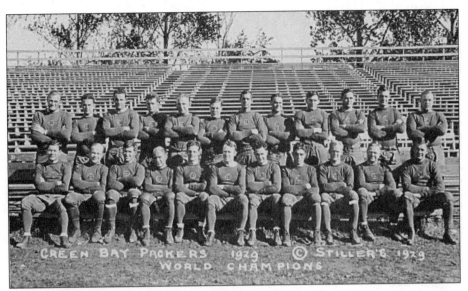

1929 team photo, b&w, 8" x 10", Stiller ($45-$60).

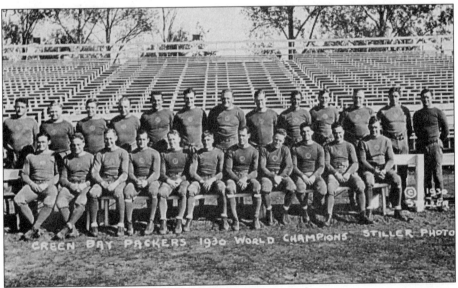

1930 team photo, b&w, 8" x 10", Stiller ($45-$65).

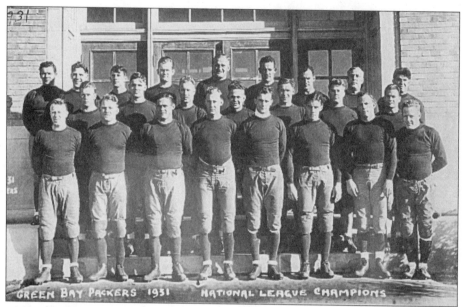

1931 team photo, b&w, 8" x 10", Stiller ($45-$65).

1932 team photo, b&w, 8" x 10", Stiller ($35-$50).

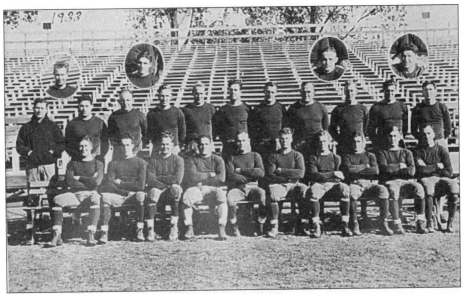

1933 team photo, b&w, 8" x 10", Stiller ($35-$50).

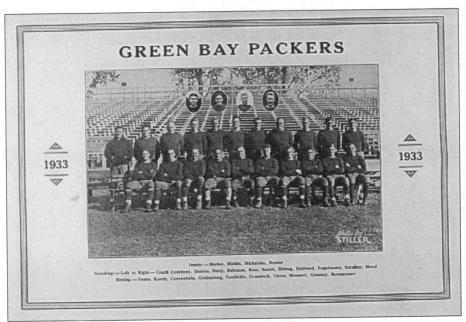

1933 team photo, b&w, Waltham giveaway ($50-$95+).

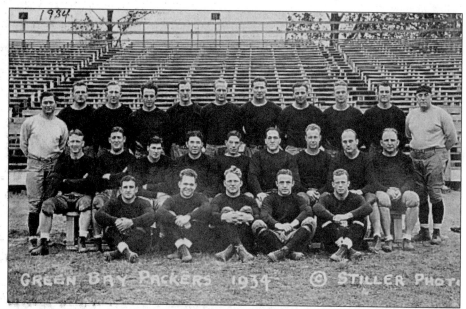

1934 team photo, b&w, 8" x 10", Stiller ($35-$50).

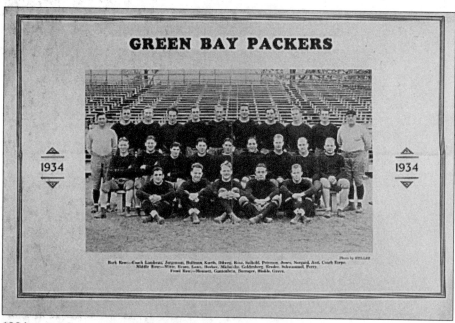

1934 team photo, b&w, Waltham giveaway ($50-$95+).

1935 team photo, b&w, 8" x 10", Stiller ($35-$50).

1936 team photo, b&w, 8" x 10", Stiller ($45-$65).

1937 team photo, b&w, 8" x 10", Stiller ($35-$50).

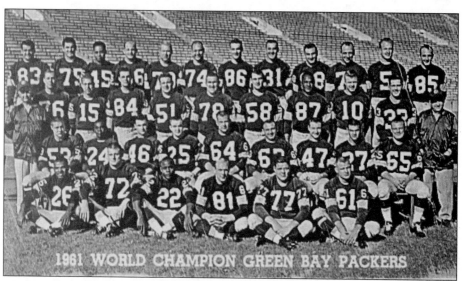

1966 team photo, b&w, 8" x 10", Super Bowl I ($15-$35).

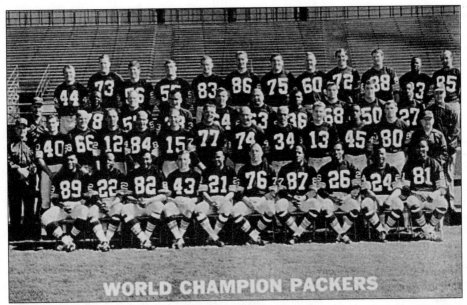

1967 team photo, b&w, 8" x 10", Super Bowl II ($15-$35).

1940s player photo with Rockwood Lodge in the background, b&w, 8" x 10" ($20-$40).

1960s game-action photo, b&w, 8" x 10" ($15-$30).

High Scoring Packers

While Don Hutson holds the scoring mark with 29 points in a single quarter (vs. Detroit, Oct. 7, 1945), with four touchdowns and five extra points, he doesn't hold the record for the most points in a game. Paul Hornung (vs. Baltimore, Oct. 8, 1961), tallied 33 points on four touchdowns, six extra points and a field goal. In Hutson's game, he added two more extra points for a total of 31 for the game.

Chapter 26

Postcards

The earliest Packers postcards are from the 1920s. Green Bay photographer Otto Stiller did the majority of the old postcards. Team photographs, game-action shots, stadium photos and individual player photos are all popular postcard subjects. Stamped postcards with a cancellation on the back are popular because they can date the postcard. Many postcards were sold for a number of years, making it difficult to determine what year they were printed. Championship team postcards and Hall of Fame player postcards should be priced at the higher end of the ranges given below.

Like all paper items, condition determines much of the price. Stains, holes, creases, tears and fading all detract from a postcard's price. Excellent condition postcards will have almost no damage and will appear to be almost new. Good-Very Good post cards will have minor damage, such as light fading or stains and small creases or pin holes. Poor-Fair condition postcards will have major damage, ranging from pieces missing to heavy stains or creases. Poor-Fair condition postcards have minimal value.

Years	*Stadium*		*Team*		*Game Action*	
1920s (rare)	25.00	100.00	20.00	75.00	20.00	75.00
1930s	20.00	75.00	15.00	50.00	15.00	50.00
1940s	15.00	45.00	10.00	35.00	10.00	30.00
1950s	10.00	35.00	8.00	25.00	10.00	25.00
1960s	8.00	25.00	10.00	30.00	8.00	20.00
1970s	5.00	15.00	4.00	10.00	3.00	10.00
1980s	3.00	10.00	3.00	8.00	2.00	8.00
1990s	1.00	5.00	1.00	5.00	1.00	5.00

Intercept This

Bobby Dillon holds the all-time Packers mark for most interceptions with 52, followed by Willie Wood with 48 and Herb Adderley with 39. Irv Comp leads the team with 10 picks in one season, while Dillon and Willie Buchanon hold the team record with four interceptions in one game.

Early 1920s postcard, b&w, real photo, game in progress, rare ($45-$75).

1929 team postcard, b&w, rare ($50-$95).

1940s stadium postcard, color ($15-$30).

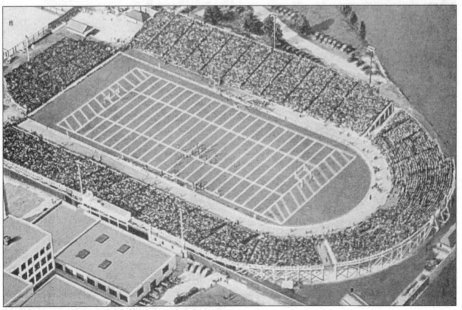

1940s stadium postcard, color ($15-$30).

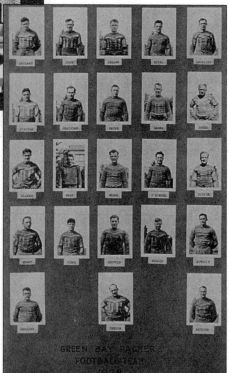

Late 1940s postcard, Don Hutson's Playdium ($15-$45).

1928 team postcard, b&w, rare ($50-$95).

1940s, "Greetings from Green Bay" postcard, stadium and player, color ($10-$25).

1940s/50s stadium postcard, b&w ($15-$30).

Early 1950s postcard, majorettes, color ($10-$20).

1960s stadium postcard, color photo ($10-$20).

1970s Bart Starr postcard, color photo ($8-$20).

1963 team postcard, color photo ($10-$20).

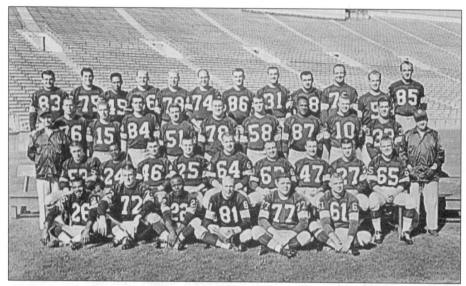

1961 postcard, color photo, no caption ($10-$25).

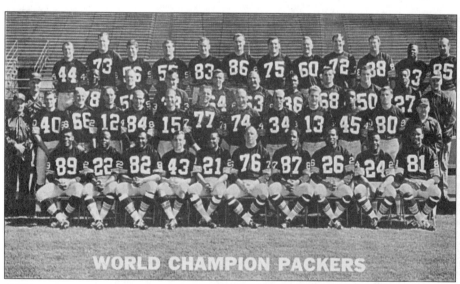

WORLD CHAMPION PACKERS

1967 team postcard, Super Bowl II, color photo ($15-$30).

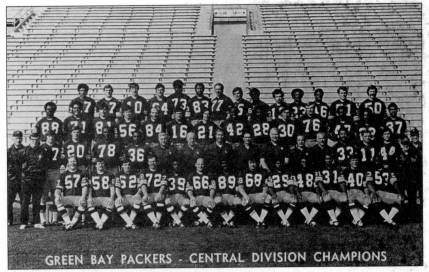

GREEN BAY PACKERS - CENTRAL DIVISION CHAMPIONS

1972 team postcard, color photo ($5-$10).

1960s Bart Starr postcard, color photo ($10-$25).

Chapter 27

Posters

Old advertising and schedule posters from the 1920s to the 1940s are a prized collectible. Many posters were thrown away. Stadium, team or players' photographs add to a poster's value. Most posters were secured by thumbtacks or tape, making condition very important in estimating value. Large color team posters sponsored by Old Style beer have been given out annually since 1978. *Sports Illustrated* also issued posters in the late 1960s and early 1970s.

Excellent condition posters will have no holes, very light creases, no tears or stains and appear almost new. Good-Very Good condition posters can have pin holes at the corners, light creases, very small tears, but no obvious stains. Poor-Fair condition posters will have major damage such as large tears, obvious stains, creases, holes, fading and writing. Posters in Poor to Fair condition have little value.

Posters

Years	*Price Range*	
1920s (rare)	50.00	250.00
1930s	40.00	200.00
1940s	35.00	175.00
1950s	30.00	150.00
1960s	25.00	125.00
1970s	10.00	45.00
1980s	5.00	30.00
1990s	3.00	20.00

Sports Illustrated Posters (1968-1971)

Player	*Price Range*	
John Brockington	10.00	20.00
Ray Nitschke	10.00	20.00
Bar Starr	10.00	35.00

1960s poster ($20-$35).

GREEN BAY PACKERS

Bart Starr poster, Jack Webb Corp., 1968 ($10-$35).

1970s - 1980's Bart Starr poster, Ice Bowl, green and gold ($5-$10)

1972 poster ($10-$25).

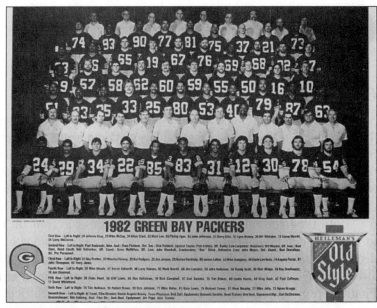

Old Style team poster, 1982 ($5-$10).

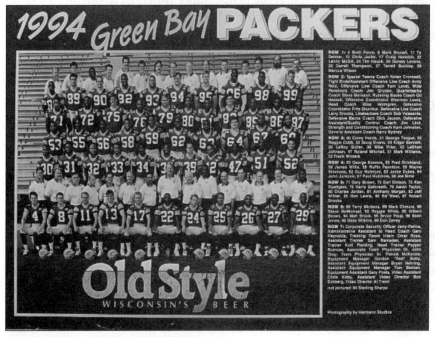

Old Style team poster, 1994 ($3-$8).

Chapter 28

Press Items

Press items are popular because of the limited number of items made and the uniqueness of the items. Pins, guides, credentials and banquet items are all becoming very collectible and valuable. Large Packers press books were issued from 1935-1946. Small media guides were issued from 1946 to the present. Many of the early game press passes were made of silk. They were colorful and pinned on the clothing. Later, the silk passes were replaced with paper passes.

Until 1964, the only way to obtain press guides was from the team. Starting in 1965 and continuing until 1979, the Wisconsin Ford automobile dealerships distributed them free of charge and made them a lot easier to find. In the early 1980s through the present, media guides could be purchased at retail outlets. Finding press items from the 1920s to the 1960s is very difficult. Most items were given out free and many press items were thrown out. Up until the first Super Bowl, there was very few press items. Super Bowls have produced lots of press items, including passes, lunch buckets, pins, guides, attaché cases and more. As with all collectibles, condition is very important and will determine part of an item's price.

Press Books

Years	*Price Range*	
1935-1946, each	50.00	125.00

Press Guides

Years	*Price Range*	
1947-1950, each	45.00	95.00
1951-1959, each	40.00	75.00
1960-1964, each	25.00	50.00
1965-1969, each	15.00	35.00
1970-1979, each	5.00	12.00
1980-1989, each	4.00	10.00
1990-1997, each	4.00	10.00

Press Passes

Year	Regular Season Games		Championship Games	
1930s	15.00	45.00	25.00	100.00
1940s	12.00	35.00	20.00	75.00
1950s	10.00	30.00	n/a	
1960s	8.00	25.00	15.00	60.00
1970s	4.00	10.00	n/a	
1980s	3.00	8.00	n/a	
1990s	2.00	8.00	10.00	40.00

Press Pins (Championship Games)

Year	Price Range	
1936	150.00	500.00
1938	150.00	550.00
1939	125.00	450.00
1944	100.00	400.00
1960	75.00	200.00
1961	50.00	150.00
1962	75.00	200.00
1965	45.00	100.00
1966	250.00	1,000.00+
1967	250.00	1,000.00+
1997	50.00	150.00

1950s silk "Gate" press ribbon, colorful, 1-1/2" x 6" ($25-$35).

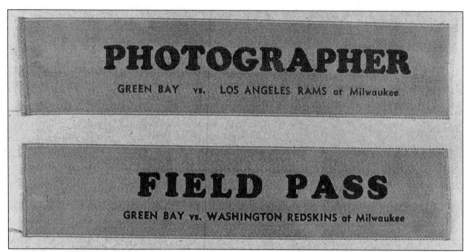

1950s silk "Photographer" and "Field Pass" press ribbons, colorful, 1-1/2" x 6" ($25-$35 each).

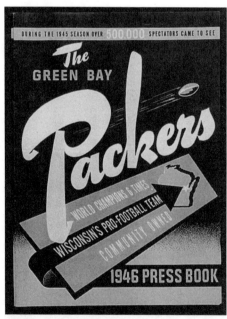

1946 Press Book ($60-$125).

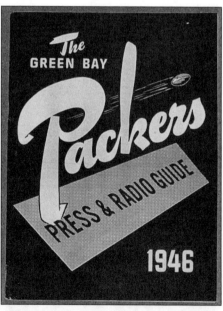

1946 Press & Radio Guide ($50-$95).

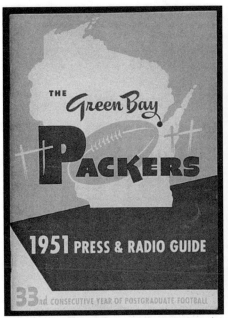

1951 Press & Radio Guide ($40-$75).

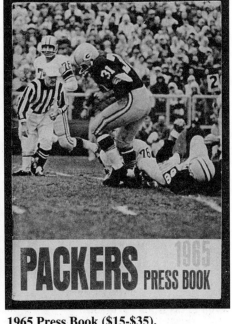

1965 Press Book ($15-$35).

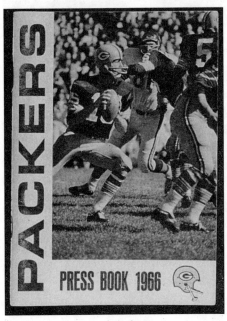

1966 Press Book ($15-$35).

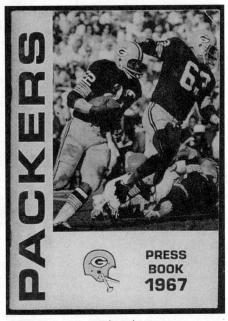

1967 Press Book ($15-$35).

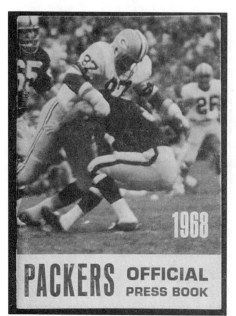

1997 Championship Game press pin ($75-$125).

1968 Press Book ($10-$30).

1980s assorted dressing-room passes, colorful ($4-$12 each).

1980s assorted press-box passes, colorful ($4-$12 each).

Chapter 29

Programs

The earliest Packers programs are the "Dope Sheets" from 1921-24. They contained a vast amount of information about the Packers and the league. Because they were printed on very thin paper, they damaged easily and are difficult to find in excellent condition. "Dope Sheets" are extremely difficult to find and are getting more valuable. During the 1920s, most programs showed full-length photographs of the players with biographies underneath. Programs from the 1920s to the 1960s had a large variety of covers that featured players, artwork and the stadium. Covers with photographs of the stadium or Hall of Famers on them command higher prices.

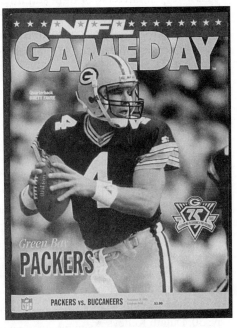

Nov. 28, 1993, Tampa Bay Buccaneers, Brett Favre cover ($8-$15).

Programs fall into three categories: pre-season, regular season and playoff or Championship. Generally, Championship and Super Bowl programs are the most valuable, with regular and pre-season being worth less. Because the NFL had no playoff system before 1933, there is no championship programs for 1929, 1930 or 1931. Games that have historical significance can increase a program's value (a player's retirement, Stadium Dedication, a record being set and a player's or coach's first or last game).

Store program's in a bag or envelope and keep them in a clean, dry place. If you are going to display them, avoid direct sunlight and handle them as little as possible. Many factors combine to determine a program's value, including the condition of the cover (creases, tears, stains and writing detract from price). Because the lineups are usually listed on the center page, make sure it isn't missing or loose. The three categories of condition are Poor-Fair, Good-Very Good and Excellent or better. Poor to Fair is complete, but has major cover and/or inside damage such as tears, heavy creasing, loose cover, obvious staining, severe fading and writing. Programs that are incomplete or missing the cover have little value. Good to Very Good is condition programs have normal wear such as light creases, very small tears or light staining. Excellent or better condition programs display little wear and will look almost new inside and out.

The prices listed vary according to condition. Cover and game importance can both increase the price. All games listed are at Green Bay, unless noted.

Date/Team	Price Range

1920
Lineup sheets only (rare)	200.00	600.00

1921
Oct. 23, Minneapolis Marines	150.00	350.00
Oct. 30, Rock Island Independents	150.00	350.00
Nov. 6, Evansville Crimson Giants	150.00	350.00

1922
Oct. 8, Racine Legion	135.00	350.00
Oct. 29, Rock Island Independents	135.00	350.00
Nov. 5, Columbus Panhandlers	150.00	350.00
Nov. 12, Minneapolis Marines	135.00	350.00
Nov. 30, Duluth Kelleys	150.00	350.00

1923
Sept. 30, Minneapolis Marines	135.00	350.00
Oct. 7, St. Louis All-Stars	150.00	350.00
Oct. 14, Chicago Bears (first game at Green Bay!)	200.00	450.00
Oct. 21, Milwaukee Badgers	150.00	350.00
Oct. 28, Racine Legion	150.00	350.00
Nov. 25, Duluth Kelleys	150.00	350.00
Nov. 29, Hammond Pros	150.00	350.00

1924
Oct. 12, Kansas City Blues	150.00	350.00
Oct. 19, Milwaukee Badgers	125.00	325.00
Oct. 26, Minneapolis Marines	150.00	350.00
Nov. 2, Racine Legion	125.00	325.00
Nov. 9, Duluth Kelleys	125.00	325.00

1925

Sept. 20, Hammond Pros	125.00	300.00
Sept. 27, Chicago Bears	150.00	350.00
Oct. 11, Chicago Cardinals	125.00	300.00
Oct. 18, Rock Island Independents	125.00	300.00
Oct. 25, Rochester Jeffersons	150.00	350.00
Nov. 25, Dayton Triangles	125.00	300.00

1926

Sept. 19, Detroit Panthers	125.00	300.00
Sept. 26, Chicago Bears	125.00	300.00
Oct. 3, Duluth Eskimos	150.00	350.00
Oct. 10, Chicago Cardinals	125.00	300.00
Oct. 17, Milwaukee Badgers	125.00	300.00
Oct. 24, Racine Tornados	150.00	350.00
Nov. 14, Louisville Colonels	150.00	350.00

1927

Sept. 18, Dayton Triangles	100.00	250.00
Sept. 25, Cleveland Bulldogs	125.00	300.00
Oct. 2, Chicago Bears	125.00	300.00
Oct. 9, Duluth Eskimos	125.00	300.00
Oct. 16, Chicago Cardinals	100.00	250.00
Oct. 23, New York Yankees	125.00	300.00
Nov. 13, Dayton Triangles	125.00	300.00

1928

Sept. 23, Frankford Yellowjackets	125.00	300.00
Sept. 30, Chicago Bears	125.00	300.00
Oct. 7, New York Giants	125.00	300.00
Oct. 14, Chicago Cardinals	100.00	250.00
Oct. 28, Dayton Triangles	125.00	300.00
Nov. 4, Pottsville Maroons	125.00	300.00
Nov. 11, New York Yankees	125.00	300.00

1929 (First Championship Year)

Sept. 22, Dayton Triangles	100.00	250.00
Sept. 29, Chicago Bears	100.00	250.00
Oct. 6, Chicago Cardinals	100.00	250.00

Oct. 13, Frankford Yellowjackets 100.00   250.00
Oct. 20, Minneapolis Redjackets 150.00   350.00

1930 (Championship Year)
Sept. 21, Chicago Cardinals 75.00   200.00
Sept. 28, Chicago Bears 75.00   200.00
Oct. 5, New York Giants 75.00   200.00
Oct. 12, Frankford Yellowjackets 75.00   200.00
Oct. 26, Minneapolis Redjackets 75.00   200.00
Nov. 2, Portsmouth Spartans 75.00   200.00

1931 (Championship Year)
Sept. 13, Cleveland Indians 75.00   200.00
Sept. 25, Brooklyn Dodgers 60.00   175.00
Sept. 27, Chicago Bears 60.00   175.00
Oct. 4, New York Giants 50.00   150.00
Oct. 11, Chicago Cardinals 50.00   150.00
Oct. 18, Frankford Yellowjackets 60.00   175.00
Oct. 25, Providence Steamrollers 60.00   175.00
Nov. 8, Staten Island Stapletons 60.00   175.00

1932
Sept. 18, Chicago Cardinals 50.00   150.00
Sept. 25, Chicago Bears 50.00   150.00
Oct. 2, New York Giants 50.00   150.00
Oct. 9, Portsmouth Spartans 50.00   150.00
Oct. 23, Brooklyn Dodgers 50.00   150.00
Oct. 30, Staten Island Stapletons 50.00   150.00

1933
Sept. 17, Boston Redskins 50.00   150.00
Sept. 24, Chicago Bears 45.00   125.00
Oct. 1, New York Giants (first Milwaukee game) 75.00   200.00
Oct. 8, Portsmouth Spartans 50.00   150.00
Oct. 15, Pittsburgh Pirates 50.00   150.00
Oct. 29, Philadelphia Eagles 50.00   150.00

1934
Sept. 16, Philadelphia Eagles 50.00   150.00

Sept. 23, Chicago Bears 45.00   125.00
Sept. 30, New York Giants (Milwaukee)................................50.00   150.00
Oct. 7, Detroit Lions 50.00   150.00
Oct. 14, Cincinnati Reds 65.00   175.00
Oct. 21, Chicago Cardinals 50.00   150.00
Nov. 18, Chicago Cardinals (Milwaukee) 50.00   150.00

1935
Sept. 15, Chicago Cardinals 45.00   125.00
Sept. 22, Chicago Bears 45.00   125.00
Sept. 29, New York Giants 45.00   125.00
Oct. 6, Pittsburgh Pirates...50.00   150.00
Oct. 13, Chicago Cardinals (Milwaukee)................................45.00   125.00
Oct. 20, Detroit Lions (Milwaukee)...45.00   125.00
Nov. 10, Detroit Lions 45.00   125.00

1936 (Championship Year)
Sept. 13, Chicago Cardinals 50.00   150.00
Sept. 20, Chicago Bears 50.00   150.00
Oct. 4, Chicago Cardinals (Milwaukee)..................................50.00   150.00
Oct. 11, Boston Redskins..50.00   150.00
Oct. 18, Detroit Lions 50.00   150.00
Oct. 25, Pittsburgh Pirates (Milwaukee)................................50.00   150.00
NFL Championship Game
Dec. 6, Boston Redskins at New York.....................................300.00   800.00+

1937
Sept. 12, Chicago Cardinals 45.00   125.00
Sept. 19, Chicago Bears 45.00   125.00
Oct. 3, Detroit Lions 45.00   125.00
Oct. 10, Chicago Cardinals (Milwaukee)................................45.00   125.00
Oct. 24, Cleveland Rams...45.00   125.00
Nov. 14, Philadelphia Eagles (Milwaukee) 45.00   125.00

1938
Sept. 11, Cleveland Rams 45.00   125.00
Sept. 18, Chicago Bears 45.00   125.00
Sept. 25, Chicago Cardinals (Milwaukee) 45.00   125.00

Oct. 9, Detroit Lions 45.00   125.00
Oct. 16, Brooklyn Dodgers (Milwaukee)................................45.00   125.00
Oct. 23, Pittsburgh Pirates...45.00   125.00
NFL Championship Game (lost to New York)
Dec. 10, New York Giants at New York ....300.00 1,500.00+

1939 (Championship Year)

Sept. 17, Chicago Cardinals...45.00   125.00
Sept. 24, Chicago Bears 45.00   125.00
Oct. 1, Cleveland Rams...45.00   125.00
Oct. 8, Chicago Cardinals (Milwaukee)................................45.00   125.00
Oct. 22, Detroit Lions 45.00   125.00
Oct. 29, Washington Redskins 45.00   125.00
NFL Championship Game
Dec. 10, New York Giants (Milwaukee) ....250.00   750.00+

1940

Sept. 15, Philadelphia Eagles...35.00   85.00
Sept. 22, Chicago Bears 35.00   85.00
Sept. 29, Chicago Cardinals (Milwaukee) 35.00   85.00
Oct. 13, Cleveland Rams...35.00   85.00
Oct. 20, Detroit Lions 35.00   85.00
Oct. 27, Pittsburgh Steelers (Milwaukee) 35.00   85.00

1941

Sept. 14, Detroit Lions 35.00   80.00
Sept. 21, Cleveland Rams 35.00   80.00
Sept. 28, Chicago Bears 35.00   80.00
Oct. 5, Chicago Cardinals (Milwaukee)..................................35.00   80.00
Oct. 12, Brooklyn Dodgers 35.00   80.00
Nov. 16, Chicago Cardinals 35.00   80.00

1942

Sept. 27, Chicago Bears 35.00   80.00
Oct. 11, Detroit Lions (Milwaukee)..35.00   80.00
Oct. 18, Cleveland Rams...35.00   80.00
Nov. 1, Chicago Cardinals 35.00   80.00
Dec. 6, Pittsburgh Steelers (Milwaukee) 45.00   100.00

1943

Sept. 26, Chicago Bears	35.00	80.00
Oct. 10, Detroit Lions	35.00	80.00
Oct. 17, Washington Redskins (Milwaukee)	35.00	80.00
Nov. 14, Chicago Cardinals (Milwaukee)	40.00	85.00

1944 (Championship Year)

Sept. 17, Brooklyn Tigers (Milwaukee)	45.00	100.00
Sept. 24, Chicago Bears	40.00	95.00
Oct. 1, Detroit Lions (Milwaukee)	45.00	95.00
Oct. 8, Card-Pitt	45.00	95.00
Oct. 22, Cleveland Rams	45.00	95.00

NFL Championship Game

Dec. 17, New York Giants at New York	250.00	650.00

1945

Sept. 30, Chicago Bears	35.00	80.00
* Oct. 7, Detroit Lions (Milwaukee)	50.00	125.00
Oct. 14, Cleveland Rams	35.00	80.00
Oct. 21, Boston Yanks (Milwaukee)	40.00	85.00
Oct. 28, Chicago Cardinals	35.00	80.00

* Don Hutson scores 29 points in 1 quarter

1946

Sept. 29, Chicago Bears	35.00	80.00
Oct. 6, Los Angeles Rams (Milwaukee)	35.00	80.00
Oct. 20, Pittsburgh Steelers	35.00	80.00
Oct. 27, Detroit Lions (Milwaukee)	35.00	80.00
Nov. 24, Chicago Cardinals	35.00	80.00

1947

Sept. 28, Chicago Bears	35.00	80.00
Oct. 5, Los Angeles Rams (Milwaukee)	35.00	80.00
Oct. 12, Chicago Cardinals	35.00	80.00
Oct. 19, Washington Redskins (Milwaukee)	35.00	80.00
Oct. 26, Detroit Lions	35.00	80.00
Nov. 2, Pittsburgh Steelers (Milwaukee)	35.00	80.00

1948

Sept. 26, Chicago Bears	35.00	80.00
Oct. 3, Detroit Lions	35.00	80.00
Oct. 10, Chicago Cardinals (Milwaukee)	35.00	80.00
Oct. 17, Los Angeles Rams	35.00	80.00
Oct. 24, Washington Redskins (Milwaukee)	35.00	80.00
Nov. 21, New York Giants (Milwaukee)	35.00	80.00

1949

Sept. 25, Chicago Bears	35.00	75.00
Oct. 2, Los Angeles Rams	35.00	75.00
Oct. 16, Chicago Cardinals (Milwaukee)	35.00	75.00
Oct. 30, Detroit Lions (Milwaukee)	35.00	75.00
* Nov. 13, New York Giants	45.00	85.00
Nov. 20, Pittsburgh Steelers (Milwaukee)	35.00	75.00

* Lambeau's Last Home Game!

1950

Sept. 17, Detroit Lions	25.00	50.00
Sept. 24, Washington Redskins (Milwaukee)	20.00	45.00
Oct. 1, Chicago Bears	20.00	45.00
Oct. 8, New York Yanks	25.00	45.00
Nov. 12, Los Angeles Rams (Milwaukee)	20.00	45.00
Nov. 26, San Francisco 49ers	20.00	45.00

1951

Sept. 30, Chicago Bears	20.00	45.00
Oct. 7, Pittsburgh Steelers (Milwaukee)	20.00	45.00
Oct. 14, Philadelphia Eagles	20.00	45.00
Oct. 21, Los Angeles Rams (Milwaukee)	20.00	45.00
Nov. 4, Detroit Lions	20.00	45.00
Dec. 2, New York Yanks	25.00	50.00

1952

Sept. 28, Chicago Bears	20.00	45.00
Oct. 5, Washington Redskins (Milwaukee)	20.00	45.00
Oct. 12, Los Angeles Rams (Milwaukee)	20.00	45.00

Nov. 2, Philadelphia Eagles (Milwaukee) 20.00   45.00
Nov. 23, Dallas Texans 30.00   55.00

1953
Sept. 27, Cleveland Browns (Milwaukee) 25.00   45.00
Oct. 4, Chicago Bears 15.00   40.00
Oct. 11, Los Angeles Rams (Milwaukee) 15.00   40.00
Oct. 18, Baltimore Colts 15.00   40.00
Nov. 15, Detroit Lions 15.00   40.00
Nov. 22, San Francisco 49ers (Milwaukee)..15.00   40.00

1954
Sept. 26, Pittsburgh Steelers 15.00   40.00
Oct. 3, Chicago Bears 15.00   40.00
Oct. 10, San Francisco 49ers (Milwaukee) 15.00   40.00
Oct. 17, Los Angeles Rams (Milwaukee) 15.00   40.00
Nov. 13, Baltimore Colts (Milwaukee)..15.00   40.00
Nov. 21, Detroit Lions 15.00   40.00

1955
Sept. 25, Detroit Lions 15.00   40.00
Oct. 2, Chicago Bears 15.00   40.00
Oct. 8, Baltimore Colts (Milwaukee)..15.00   40.00
Oct. 16, Los Angeles Rams (Milwaukee) 15.00   40.00
Nov. 13, Chicago Cardinals 15.00   40.00
Nov. 20, San Francisco 49ers (Milwaukee)..15.00   40.00

1956
Sept. 30, Detroit Lions 12.00   30.00
Oct. 7, Chicago Bears 12.00   30.00
Oct. 14, Baltimore Colts (Milwaukee)..12.00   30.00
Oct. 21, Los Angeles Rams (Milwaukee) 12.00   30.00
Nov. 4, Cleveland Browns (Milwaukee) 12.00   30.00
Nov. 18, San Francisco 49ers...12.00   30.00

1957
*Sept. 29, Chicago Bears (Stadium Dedication)....................................40.00   75.00
Oct. 6, Detroit Lions 12.00   30.00
Oct. 13, Baltimore Colts (Milwaukee)..12.00   30.00

161

Oct. 20, San Francisco 49ers (Milwaukee) 12.00   30.00
Nov. 3, New York Giants...12.00   30.00
Nov. 17, Los Angeles Rams (Milwaukee)..12.00   30.00

1958

Sept. 28, Chicago Bears 12.00   30.00
Oct. 5, Detroit Lions 12.00   30.00
Oct. 12, Baltimore Colts (Milwaukee)..12.00   30.00
Oct. 26, Philadelphia Eagles 12.00   30.00
Nov. 16, Los Angeles Rams...12.00   30.00
Nov. 23, San Francisco 49ers (Milwaukee)..12.00   30.00

1959

* Sept. 27, Chicago Bears 30.00   60.00
Oct. 4, Detroit Lions 12.00   30.00
Oct. 11, San Francisco 49ers...12.00   30.00
Oct. 18, Los Angeles Rams (Milwaukee) 12.00   30.00
Nov. 15, Baltimore Colts (Milwaukee)..12.00   30.00
Nov. 22, Washington Redskins..12.00   30.00
* Lombardi's 1st Game

1960

Sept. 25, Chicago Bears 10.00   25.00
Oct. 2, Detroit Lions 10.00   25.00
Oct. 9, Baltimore Colts 10.00   25.00
Oct. 23, San Francisco 49ers (Milwaukee)..10.00   25.00
Nov. 13, Dallas Cowboys 10.00   25.00
Nov. 20, Los Angeles Rams (Milwaukee)..10.00   25.00
Dec. 26, at Philadelphia Eagles (Championship)....................................75.00   200.00

1961 (Championship Year)

Sept. 17, Detroit Lions (Milwaukee) 10.00   25.00
Sept. 24, San Francisco 49ers 10.00   25.00
Oct. 1, Chicago Bears 10.00   25.00
* Oct. 8, Baltimore Colts 15.00   25.00
Oct. 29, Minnesota Vikings (Milwaukee)..10.00   25.00
Nov. 19, Los Angeles Rams...10.00   25.00
Dec. 3, New York Giants (Milwaukee) 10.00   25.00

Dec. 31, New York Giants (Championship at Green Bay).....................50.00   175.00
* Paul Hornung scores 33 points in one game!

1962 (Championship Year)
Sept. 16, Minnesota Vikings...10.00   25.00
Sept. 23, St. Louis Cardinals (Milwaukee)..10.00   25.00
Sept. 30, Chicago Bears..10.00   25.00
Oct. 7, Detroit Lions 10.00   25.00
Oct. 21, San Francisco 49ers (Milwaukee)...10.00   25.00
Nov. 18, Baltimore Colts 10.00   25.00
Dec. 2, Los Angeles Rams (Milwaukee)..10.00   25.00
Dec. 30, at New York Giants (Championship) 75.00   200.00

1963
Sept. 15, Chicago Bears..8.00   20.00
Sept. 22, Detroit Lions (Milwaukee) 8.00   20.00
Sept. 29, Baltimore Colts 8.00   20.00
Oct. 6, Los Angeles Rams...8.00   20.00
Nov. 3, Pittsburgh Steelers (Milwaukee) 8.00   20.00
Nov. 10, Minnesota Vikings 8.00   20.00
Nov. 24, San Francisco 49ers (Milwaukee)..8.00   20.00
Jan. 5, Cleveland Browns (Playoff Bowl at Miami)..............................20.00   50.00

1964
Sept. 13, Chicago Bears 8.00   20.00
Sept. 20, Baltimore Colts 8.00   20.00
Oct. 4, Minnesota Vikings 8.00   20.00
Oct. 11, San Francisco 49ers (Milwaukee)..8.00   20.00
Oct. 25, Los Angeles Rams (Milwaukee)..8.00   20.00
Nov. 8, Detroit Lions 8.00   20.00
Nov. 22, Cleveland Browns (Milwaukee) 8.00   20.00
Jan. 3, St. Louis Cardinals (Playoff Bowl at Miami)............................20.00   50.00

1965 (Championship Year)
Sept. 26, Baltimore Colts (Milwaukee) 10.00   20.00
Oct. 3, Chicago Bears 10.00   20.00
Oct. 10, San Francisco 49ers...10.00   20.00
Oct. 24, Dallas Cowboys (Milwaukee)..10.00   20.00
Nov. 7, Detroit Lions 10.00   20.00

Nov. 14, Los Angeles Rams (Milwaukee) 10.00   20.00
Dec. 5, Minnesota Vikings...10.00   20.00
* Dec. 26, Baltimore Colts (Western Conference
Championship at Green Bay)...40.00   100.00+
Jan. 2, Cleveland Browns (Championship at Green Bay)......................75.00   200.00
* *Phantom Field Goal Game*

1966 (Super Bowl Year)

Sept. 10, Baltimore Colts (Milwaukee) 10.00   20.00
Sept. 25, Los Angeles Rams 10.00   20.00
Oct. 2, Detroit Lions 10.00   20.00
Oct. 23, Atlanta Falcons (Milwaukee) 10.00   20.00
Nov. 6, Minnesota Vikings 10.00   20.00
Nov. 20, Chicago Bears 10.00   20.00
Dec. 4, San Francisco 49ers (Milwaukee) 10.00   20.00
Jan. 1, at Dallas Cowboys (Championship) 45.00   150.00
Jan. 15, Kansas City Chiefs (Super Bowl I at Los Angeles) 100.00   300.00

1967 (Super Bowl Year)

Sept. 17, Detroit Lions 10.00   20.00
Sept. 24, Chicago Bears 10.00   20.00
Oct. 1, Atlanta Falcons (Milwaukee) 10.00   20.00
Oct. 15, Minnesota Vikings (Milwaukee)...10.00   20.00
Nov. 12, Cleveland Browns (Milwaukee) 10.00   20.00
Nov. 19, San Francisco 49ers...10.00   20.00
Dec. 17, Pittsburgh Steelers 10.00   20.00
Dec. 23, Los Angeles Rams (Western Conference
   Championship at Milwaukee) 25.00   70.00
* Dec. 31, Dallas Cowboys (Championship at Green Bay)..................100.00   250.00
Jan. 14, Oakland Raiders (Super Bowl II at Miami)...........................100.00   300.00
* *Ice Bowl*

1968

Sept. 15, Philadelphia Eagles 4.00   10.00
Sept. 22, Minnesota Vikings (Milwaukee) 4.00   10.00
Sept. 29, Detroit Lions 4.00   10.00
Oct. 13, Los Angeles Rams (Milwaukee) 4.00   10.00

Nov. 3, Chicago Bears 4.00   10.00
Nov. 17, New Orleans Saints (Milwaukee) 4.00   10.00
Dec. 7, Baltimore Colts..4.00   10.00

1969

Sept. 21, Chicago Bears 4.00   10.00
Sept. 28, San Francisco 49ers 4.00   10.00
Oct. 26, Atlanta Falcons...4.00   10.00
Nov. 16, Minnesota Vikings (Milwaukee)...4.00   10.00
Nov. 23, Detroit Lions 4.00   10.00
Nov. 30, New York Giants (Milwaukee)..4.00   10.00
Dec. 21, St. Louis Cardinals 4.00   10.00

1970

Sept. 20, Detroit Lions 3.00   8.00
Sept. 27, Atlanta Falcons 3.00   8.00
Oct. 4, Minnesota Vikings (Milwaukee)..3.00   8.00
* Oct. 18, Los Angeles Rams...7.00   20.00
Oct. 25, Philadelphia Eagles (Milwaukee)..3.00   8.00
Nov. 9, Baltimore Colts (Milwaukee)..3.00   8.00
Nov. 15, Chicago Bears 3.00   8.00
* *Bart Starr Day w/ insert*

1971

Sept. 19, New York Giants 3.00   8.00
Sept. 26, Denver Broncos (Milwaukee)...3.00   8.00
Oct. 3, Cincinnati Bengals 3.00   8.00
Oct. 17, Minnesota Vikings 3.00   8.00
Nov. 1, Detroit Lions (Milwaukee)..3.00   8.00
Nov. 28, New Orleans Saints (Milwaukee) 3.00   8.00
* Dec. 12, Chicago Bears...7.00   20.00
* *Ray Nitchske Day*

1972

Sept. 24, Oakland Raiders..3.00   8.00
Oct. 1, Dallas Cowboys (Milwaukee)...3.00   8.00
Oct. 8, Chicago Bears 3.00   8.00
Oct. 22, Atlanta Falcons (Milwaukee)...3.00   8.00

Oct. 29, Minnesota Vikings 3.00   8.00
Nov. 5, San Francisco 49ers (Milwaukee) 3.00   8.00
Dec. 3, Detroit Lions...3.00   8.00
Dec. 24, at Washington Redskins (Divisional Playoff) 15.00   45.00

1973
Sept. 17, New York Jets (Milwaukee) 3.00   8.00
Sept. 23, Detroit Lions 3.00   8.00
Oct. 14, Kansas City Chiefs (Milwaukee) 3.00   8.00
Nov. 4, Chicago Bears 3.00   8.00
Nov. 11, St. Louis Cardinals 3.00   8.00
Dec. 2, New Orleans Saints (Milwaukee).....................................3.00   8.00
Dec. 8, Minnesota Vikings...3.00   8.00

1974
Sept. 15, Minnesota Vikings 3.00   8.00
Sept. 29, Detroit Lions (Milwaukee) 3.00   8.00
Oct. 6, Buffalo Bills 3.00   8.00
Oct. 13, Los Angeles Rams...3.00   8.00
Nov. 3, Washington Redskins...3.00   8.00
Nov. 10, Chicago Bears (Milwaukee)..3.00   8.00
Nov. 24, San Diego Chargers...3.00   8.00

1975
Sept. 21, Detroit Lions (Milwaukee) 3.00   8.00
Oct. 5, Miami Dolphins..3.00   8.00
Oct. 26, Pittsburgh Steelers (Milwaukee) 3.00   8.00
Nov. 2, Minnesota Vikings 3.00   8.00
Nov. 23, New York Giants (Milwaukee)..3.00   8.00
Nov. 30, Chicago Bears 3.00   8.00
Dec. 21, Atlanta Falcons 3.00   8.00

1976
Sept. 12, San Francisco 49ers 3.00   8.00
Oct. 3, Detroit Lions 3.00   8.00
Oct. 10, Seattle Seahawks (Milwaukee) 3.00   8.00
Oct. 17, Philadelphia Eagles 3.00   8.00

Nov. 7, New Orleans Saints (Milwaukee) 3.00   8.00
Nov. 21, Minnesota Vikings (Milwaukee)..3.00   8.00
Nov. 28, Chicago Bears 3.00   8.00

1977
Sept. 25, Houston Oilers 3.00   8.00
Oct. 9, Cincinnati Bengals (Milwaukee)..3.00   8.00
Oct. 30, Chicago Bears 3.00   8.00
Nov. 13, Los Angeles Rams (Milwaukee)..3.00   8.00
Nov. 27, Minnesota Vikings 3.00   8.00
Dec. 4, Detroit Lions..3.00   8.00
Dec. 18, San Francisco 49ers (Milwaukee) 3.00   8.00

1978
Sept. 10, New Orleans Saints (Milwaukee) 3.00   8.00
Sept. 17, Oakland Raiders..3.00   10.00
Oct. 1, Detroit Lions (Milwaukee)...3.00   8.00
Oct. 8, Chicago Bears 3.00   8.00
Oct. 15, Seattle Seahawks (Milwaukee) 3.00   8.00
Oct. 29, Tampa Bay Buccaneers 3.00   8.00
Nov. 12, Dallas Cowboys (Milwaukee)..3.00   10.00
Nov. 26, Minnesota Vikings 3.00   8.00

1979
Sept. 9, New Orleans Saints (Milwaukee) 3.00   8.00
Sept. 16, Tampa Bay Buccaneers..3.00   8.00
Oct. 1, New England Patriots..3.00   8.00
Oct. 14, Detroit Lions (Milwaukee)...3.00   8.00
Nov. 4, New York Jets 3.00   8.00
Nov. 11, Minnesota Vikings (Milwaukee)..3.00   8.00
Nov. 25, Philadelphia Eagles 3.00   8.00
Dec. 9, Chicago Bears..3.00   8.00

1980
Sept. 7, Chicago Bears 2.00   7.00
Sept. 14, Detroit Lions (Milwaukee) 2.00   7.00
Sept. 28, Dallas Cowboys (Milwaukee)...2.00   7.00
Oct. 5, Cincinnati Bengals 2.00   7.00
Oct. 26, Minnesota Vikings 2.00   7.00

Nov. 9, San Francisco 49ers..2.00   7.00
Nov. 30, Tampa Bay Buccaneers (Milwaukee) 2.00   7.00
Dec. 14, Houston Oilers..2.00   7.00

1981

Sept. 13, Atlanta Falcons 2.00   7.00
Sept. 27, Minnesota Vikings (Milwaukee) 2.00   7.00
Oct. 11, Tampa Bay Buccaneers..2.00   7.00
Oct. 18, San Francisco 49ers (Milwaukee) 2.00   7.00
Nov. 1, Seattle Seahawks..2.00   7.00
Nov. 8, New York Giants (Milwaukee)...2.00   7.00
Nov. 15, Chicago Bears 2.00   7.00
Dec. 6, Detroit Lions..2.00   7.00

1982 (Strike Shortened Year)

Sept. 12, Los Angeles Rams (Milwaukee)..3.00   9.00
Nov. 21, Minnesota Vikings (Milwaukee)..3.00   9.00
Dec. 5, Buffalo Bills (Milwaukee)...3.00   9.00
Dec. 12, Detroit Lions..3.00   9.00

1983

Sept. 11, Pittsburgh Steelers 2.00   7.00
Sept. 18, Los Angeles Rams (Milwaukee)..2.00   7.00
Oct. 2, Tampa Bay Buccaneers..2.00   7.00
Oct. 17, Washington Redskins (Monday Night).....................................4.00   12.00
Oct. 23, Minnesota Vikings 2.00   7.00
Nov. 6, Cleveland Browns (Milwaukee) 2.00   7.00
Nov. 20, Detroit Lions (Milwaukee)..2.00   7.00
Dec. 4, Chicago Bears..2.00   7.00

1984

Sept. 2, St. Louis Cardinals..2.00   7.00
Sept. 16, Chicago Bears 2.00   7.00
Oct. 7, San Diego Chargers...2.00   7.00
Oct. 21, Seattle Seahawks (Milwaukee) 2.00   7.00
Oct. 28, Detroit Lions 2.00   7.00
Nov. 11, Minnesota Vikings (Milwaukee)..2.00   7.00

Nov. 18, Los Angeles Rams (Milwaukee) 2.00   7.00
Dec. 2, Tampa Bay Buccaneers 2.00   7.00

1985
Sept. 15, New York Giants 2.00   6.00
Sept. 22, New York Jets (Milwaukee) 2.00   6.00
Oct. 6, Detroit Lions 2.00   6.00
Oct. 13, Minnesota Vikings (Milwaukee)...2.00   6.00
Nov. 3, Chicago Bears 2.00   6.00
Nov. 17, New Orleans Saints (Milwaukee) 2.00   6.00
Dec. 1, Tampa Bay Buccaneers 2.00   6.00
Dec. 8, Miami Dolphins (Marino Cover)..4.00   12.00

1986
Sept. 7, Houston Oilers 2.00   6.00
Sept. 22, Chicago Bears 2.00   6.00
Oct. 5, Cincinnati Bengals (Milwaukee)..2.00   6.00
Oct. 12, Detroit Lions 2.00   6.00
Oct. 26, San Francisco 49ers (Milwaukee) 2.00   6.00
Nov. 9, Washington Redskins..2.00   6.00
Nov. 16, Tampa Bay Buccaneers (Milwaukee) 2.00   6.00
Dec. 7, Minnesota Vikings...2.00   6.00

1987
Sept. 13, Los Angeles Raiders 2.00   6.00
Sept. 20, Denver Broncos (Milwaukee)...3.00   8.00
Oct. 11, Detroit Lions 2.00   6.00
Oct. 18, Philadelphia Eagles 2.00   6.00
Nov. 1, Tampa Bay Buccaneers (Milwaukee) 2.00   6.00
Nov. 8, Chicago Bears 2.00   6.00
Dec. 6, San Francisco 49ers 2.00   6.00
Dec. 13, Minnesota Vikings (Milwaukee)...2.00   6.00

1988
Sept. 4, Los Angeles Rams 2.00   6.00
Sept. 11, Tampa Bay Buccaneers...2.00   6.00
Sept. 25, Chicago Bears 2.00   6.00
Oct. 9, New England Patriots (Milwaukee) 2.00   6.00
Oct. 23, Washington Redskins (Milwaukee) 2.00   6.00

Nov. 13, Indianapolis Colts..2.00   6.00
Nov. 20, Detroit Lions (Milwaukee)...2.00   6.00
Dec. 11, Minnesota Vikings...2.00   6.00

1989

Sept. 10, Tampa Bay Buccaneers..2.00   6.00
Sept. 17, New Orleans Saints...2.00   6.00
Oct. 1, Atlanta Falcons (Milwaukee) 2.00   6.00
Oct. 8, Dallas Cowboys...3.00   8.00
Oct. 29, Detroit Lions (Milwaukee)..2.00   6.00
Nov. 5, Chicago Bears 2.00   6.00
Nov. 26, Minnesota Vikings (Milwaukee).................................2.00   6.00
Dec. 10, Kansas City Chiefs 2.00   6.00

1990

Sept. 9, Los Angeles Rams 2.00   6.00
Sept. 16, Chicago Bears 2.00   6.00
Sept. 23, Kansas City Chiefs...2.00   6.00
Oct. 28, Minnesota Vikings (Milwaukee)..................................2.00   6.00
Nov. 4, San Francisco 49ers..2.00   6.00
Nov. 25, Tampa Bay Buccaneers (Milwaukee) 2.00   6.00
Dec. 9, Seattle Seahawks (Milwaukee)......................................2.00   6.00
Dec. 22, Detroit Lions...2.00   6.00

1991

Sept. 1, Philadelphia Eagles..2.00   6.00
Sept. 15, Tampa Bay Buccaneers..2.00   6.00
Oct. 6, Dallas Cowboys (Milwaukee).......................................3.00   8.00
Oct. 17, Chicago Bears 2.00   6.00
Nov. 10, Buffalo Bills (Milwaukee) 2.00   6.00
Nov. 17, Minnesota Vikings 2.00   6.00
Nov. 24, Indianapolis Colts (Milwaukee).................................2.00   6.00
Dec. 15, Detroit Lions...2.00   6.00

1992

* Sept. 6, Minnesota Vikings 5.00   15.00
Sept. 20, Cincinnati Bengals 3.00   10.00
** Sept. 27, Pittsburgh Steelers 5.00   20.00

Oct. 25, Chicago Bears 3.00   10.00
Nov. 15, Philadelphia Eagles (Milwaukee) 3.00   10.00
Nov. 29, Tampa Bay Buccaneers (Milwaukee) 3.00   10.00
Dec. 6, Detroit Lions (Milwaukee) 3.00   10.00
Dec. 20, Los Angeles Rams 3.00   10.00
* Holmgren's first Game
** Favre's first NFL Start

1993

Sept. 5, Los Angeles Rams (Milwaukee)..3.00   8.00
Sept. 12, Philadelphia Eagles 3.00   8.00
Oct. 10, Denver Broncos...3.00   8.00
Oct. 31, Chicago Bears 3.00   8.00
Nov. 21, Detroit Lions (Milwaukee)...3.00   8.00
Nov. 28, Tampa Bay Buccaneers...3.00   8.00
Dec. 19, Minnesota Vikings (Milwaukee) 3.00   8.00
Jan. 8, at Detroit Lions (Wild Card Playoff)................................15.00   30.00
Jan. 16, at Dallas Cowboys (Divisional Playoff) 15.00   30.00

1994

Sept. 4, Minnesota Vikings 3.00   8.00
Sept. 11, Miami Dolphins (Milwaukee)...3.00   8.00
Sept. 25, Tampa Bay Buccaneers...3.00   8.00
Oct. 9, Los Angeles Rams...3.00   8.00
Nov. 6, Detroit Lions (Milwaukee)..3.00   8.00
Nov. 13, New York Jets 3.00   8.00
Dec. 11, Chicago Bears..3.00   8.00
Dec. 18, Atlanta Falcons (Last Game in Milwaukee)............................15.00   35.00
Dec. 31, Detroit Lions (Wild Card Playoff at Green Bay) 15.00   35.00
Jan. 8, at Dallas Cowboys (Divisional Playoff) 15.00   30.00

1995

Sept. 3, St. Louis Rams...3.00   8.00
Sept. 17, New York Giants 3.00   8.00
Oct. 15, Detroit Lions 3.00   8.00
Oct. 22, Minnesota Vikings 3.00   8.00
Nov. 12, Chicago Bears 3.00   8.00
Nov. 26, Tampa Bay Buccaneers...3.00   8.00
Dec. 3, Cincinnati Bengals..3.00   8.00
Dec. 24, Pittsburgh Steelers 3.00   8.00

Dec. 31, Atlanta Falcons (Wild Card Playoff)	10.00	30.00
Jan. 6, at San Francisco 49ers (Divisional Playoff)	15.00	35.00
Jan. 14, at Dallas Cowboys (Championship)	15.00	30.00

1996

Sept. 9, Philadelphia Eagles	5.00	15.00
Sept. 15, San Diego Chargers	5.00	15.00
Oct. 14, San Francisco 49ers	5.00	15.00
Oct. 27, Tampa Bay Buccaneers	5.00	15.00
Nov. 3, Detroit Lions	5.00	15.00
Dec. 1, Chicago Bears	5.00	15.00
Dec. 8, Denver Broncos	5.00	15.00
Dec. 22, Minnesota Vikings	5.00	15.00
Jan. 4, San Francisco, NFC Playoff (Mud Bowl)	15.00	40.00
Jan. 12, Panthers, NFC Championship (Ice Bowl II)	15.00	35.00
Jan. 26, Patriots, Super Bowl XXXI (no bar code)	10.00	15.00

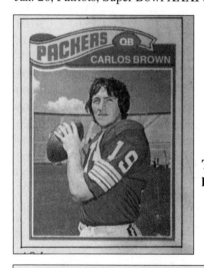

This is Carlos Brown (Alan Autry) as he appeared on his 1977 Topps card, #104.

Packer-Turned-Actor

Carlos Brown, a backup quarterback for the Packers from 1975-1976, is actor Alan Autry who played Bubba Skinner on the hit TV show "In the Heat of the Night," from 1988-1994. This former Packer has appeared in movies such as "Remember My Name," "North Dallas Forty," "Southern Comfort" and "Brewster's Millions." He also starred in "Grace Under Fire" from 1995-1996.

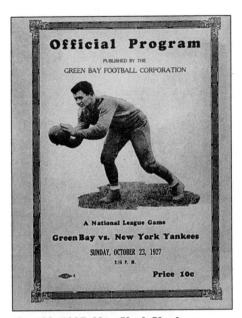

Oct. 23, 1927, New York Yankees ($125-$300).

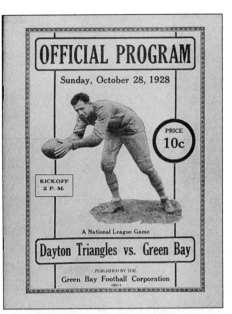

Oct. 28, 1928, Dayton Triangles ($125-$300).

Sept. 24, 1933, Chicago Bears ($45-$125).

Sept. 22, 1940, Chicago Bears ($35-$85).

Sept. 27, 1942, Chicago Bears ($35-$80).

Oct. 27, 1946, Detroit Lions at Milwaukee ($35-$80).

Sept. 26, 1948, Chicago Bears ($35-$80).

Sept. 25, 1949, Chicago Bears ($35-$75).

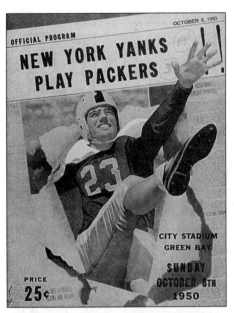

Oct. 8, 1950, New York Yanks ($20-$45).

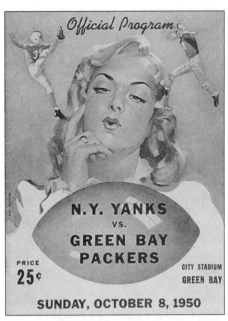

Oct. 8, 1950, New York Yanks ($20-$45).

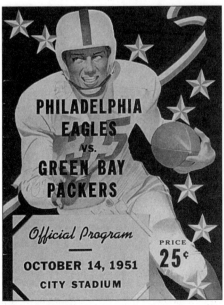

Oct. 14, 1951, Philadelphia Eagles ($20-$40).

Nov. 23, 1952, Dallas Texans ($20-$45).

Oct. 4, 1953, Chicago Bears ($15-$40).

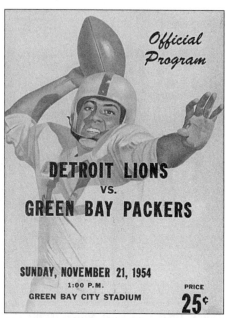

Nov. 21, 1954, Detroit Lions ($15-$35).

Nov. 13, 1955, Chicago Cardinals ($15-$35).

Sept. 29, 1957, Chicago Bears, stadium dedication ($25-$75).

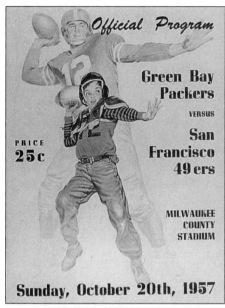

Oct. 20, 1957, San Francisco 49ers at Milwaukee ($12-$30).

Sept. 28, 1958, Chicago Bears ($12-$30).

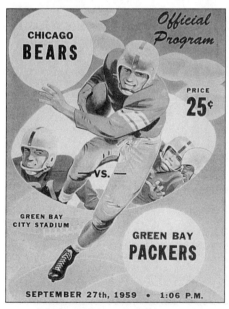

Sept. 27, 1959, Chicago Bears, Lombardi's first Game ($25-$50+).

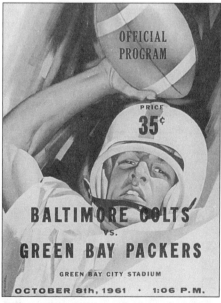

Oct. 8, 1961, Baltimore Colts ($15-$30).

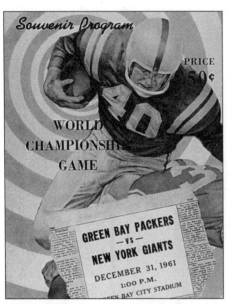

1961 NFL Championship game, Dec. 31, 1961, New York Giants at Green Bay ($50-$175).

Oct. 21, 1962, San Francisco 49ers at Milwaukee ($10-$25).

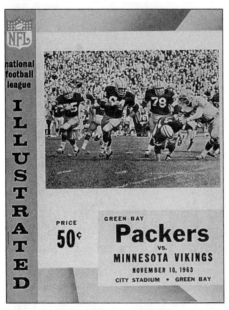

Nov. 10, 1963, Minnesota Vikings ($10-$25).

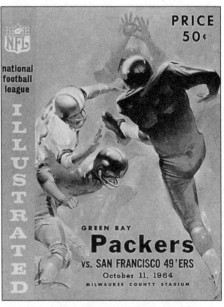

Oct. 11, 1964, San Francisco 49ers at Milwaukee ($8-$20).

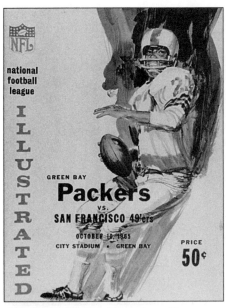

Oct. 10, 1965, San Francisco 49ers ($10-$20).

NFL Championship game, Jan. 2, 1966 at Green Bay ($75-$200).

Sept. 25, 1966, Los Angeles Rams ($10-$20).

Super Bowl I, Jan 15, 1967, vs. Kansas City Chiefs at Los Angeles ($100-$300).

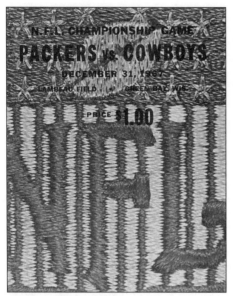

NFL Championship Game (Ice Bowl), Dec. 31, 1967, Dallas Cowboys at Green Bay ($100-$250).

Super Bowl II, Jan. 14, 1968, vs. Oakland Raiders at Miami ($100-$300).

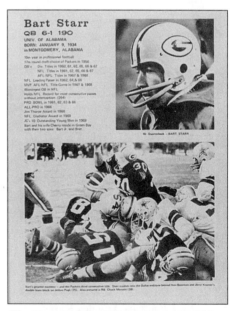

Oct. 18, 1970, Los Angeles Rams, with Bart Starr insert ($7-$20).

First page of Bart Starr insert in Oct. 18, 1970, program ($7-$20).

Dec. 12, 1971, Chicago Bears, with Ray Nitschke insert ($7-$20).

First page of Ray Nitschke insert in Dec. 12, 1971, program ($7-$20).

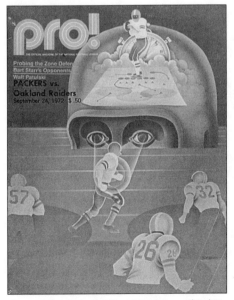

Sept. 24, 1972, Oakland Raiders ($3-$8).

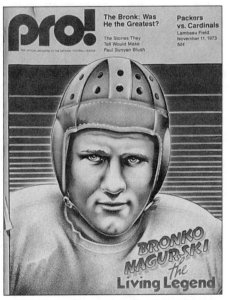

Nov. 11, 1973, St. Louis Cardinals ($3-$8).

Nov. 30, 1975, Chicago Bears ($3-$8).

Sept. 16, 1979, Tampa Bay Buccaneers ($6-$15).

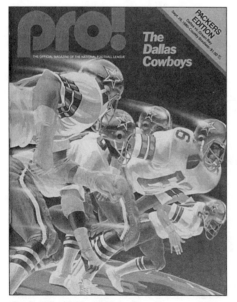

Sept. 28, 1980, Dallas Cowboys at Milwaukee ($2-$7).

Nov. 15, 1981, Chicago Bears ($2-$7).

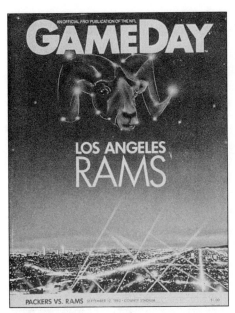

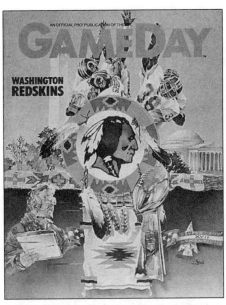

Sept. 12, 1982, Los Angeles Rams at Milwaukee ($3-$9).

Oct. 17, 1983, Washington Redskins, Monday Night ($4-$12).

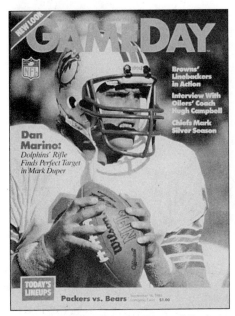

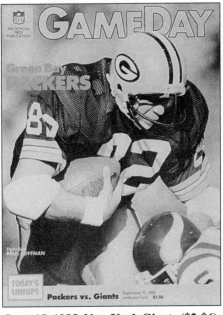

Sept. 16, 1984, Chicago Bears, Marino cover ($4-$9).

Sept. 15, 1985, New York Giants ($2-$6).

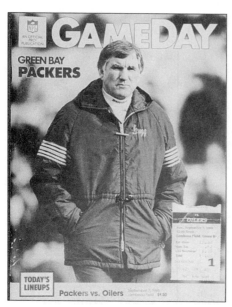

Sept. 7, 1986, Houston Oilers ($2-$6).

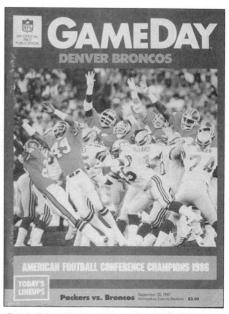

Sept. 20, 1987, Denver Broncos at Milwaukee ($3-$8).

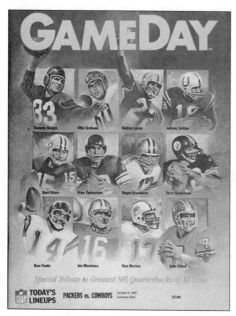

Oct. 8, 1989, Dallas Cowboys ($3-$8).

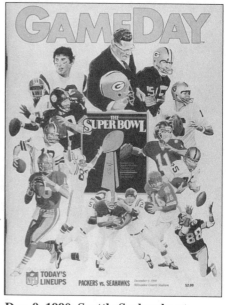

Dec. 9, 1990, Seattle Seahawks at Milwaukee ($2-$6).

Oct. 17, 1991 Chicago Bears ($2-$6).

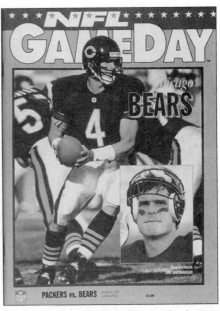

Oct. 25, 1992, Chicago Bears ($3-$10).

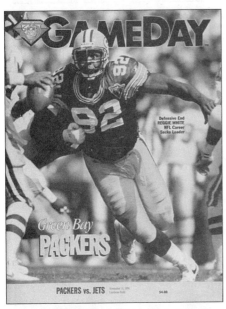

Nov. 13, 1994, New York Jets, Reggie White cover ($7-$15).

Dec. 18, 1994, Atlanta Falcons, last Milwaukee game ($15-$40).

Nov. 11, 1928, New York Yankees ($125-$300).

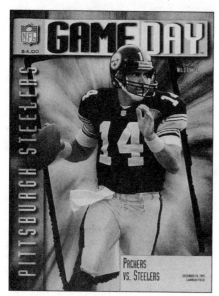

Dec. 24, 1995, Pittsburgh Steelers ($4-$10).

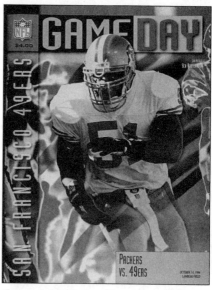

Oct. 14, 1996, San Francisco 49ers ($5-$15).

Chapter 30

Records and Tapes

Collecting audio tapes of Packers games has become very popular. It allows a person to hear a game while driving or relaxing. Championship games are the most popular. Record albums and 45s are collected both for the record itself and, in some cases, the jacket or record cover displays a photograph of a team or player. The "Glory Years" record narrated by Ted Moore chronicles the 1965, 1966 and 1967 Championship seasons. "Glory Years" is a very popular record. In 1969, a Packers Christmas Album called "Holiday Half-time" was recorded. The cartoon cover makes it a

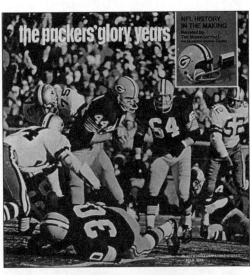

1968 record, "The Packers' Glory Years," 1965-1967 ($10-$35).

unique collectible. "Auld Lang Sine," "Jingle Bells," "Deck the Halls" and other Christmas songs are belted out in true holiday fun and spirit. Super Value food stores gave out a small thin series of records in 1962. There was one promotional record and a series of six individual records. Starr, Taylor, Moore, Currie, Kramer and Ringo each had an individual record with a color photo on the cover. The Super Bowl Stomp came out in 1968. This 45 RPM record has a plain cover. Condition of records and the record jacket are important in assessing value. Completeness of game tapes and the quality of the recording are major factors in determining an audio tape's price.

Records/Audio Tapes   *Price Range*

1930s	35.00	200.00
1940s	30.00	150.00
1950s	25.00	100.00

1960s	20.00	75.00
1970s	10.00	50.00
1980s	5.00	35.00
1990s	5.00	20.00
1967 Super Bowl Stomp (45 RPM)	15.00	45.00
1968 Glory Years Record (1965-1967)	10.00	35.00
1969 Packers Sing Holiday Halftime	10.00	35.00
1962 Super Value set (Starr, Taylor, Hornung, Currie, Kramer), set of 6	75.00	200.00

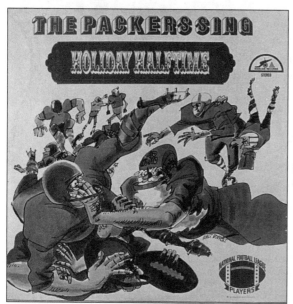

1969 record, "The Packers Sing Holiday Halftime," ($10-$35).

100-Yard Receiving Games

In 1995, Robert Brooks had nine different game in which he caught passes for more than 100 yards. That is a team record. Sterling Sharpe turned the trick seven times in 1992. James Lofton holds the all-time mark in this category with 32; Sharpe has 29.

Chapter 31

Schedules

Collecting schedules is challenging and fun. Schedules are found on a large array of items. Posters, tokens, glasses, rulers, playing cards, business cards, shopping bags, calendars, pens and pencils all had schedules on them. Finding schedules from the 1920s to the 1950s is difficult. Most items that schedules were printed on were intended to be thrown away at the end of the season. A large number of advertising schedules show the name of a person, business or a product on them. Banks, politicians, clothing stores, breweries, grocers, printers and many other companies issued items with schedules printed on them. When a team or player is pictured on the item, this ads to the value of the schedule. Add extra value if the schedule is from a championship year (1929, 1930, 1931, 1936, 1939, 1944, 1961, 1962, 1965, 1966, 1967, 1996).

1936 pocket schedule, front, Stiefel's Clothing, championship year ($25-$45).

Year	_Price Range_	
1920s (rare)	35.00	100.00
1930s	25.00	75.00
1940s	20.00	50.00
1950s	10.00	35.00
1960s	8.00	30.00
1970s	3.00	12.00
1980s	2.00	8.00
1990s	1.00	4.00

1953 token schedule, Miller Beer, aluminum ($15-$35).

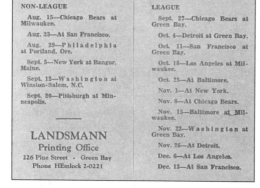

NON-LEAGUE

   Aug. 15—Chicago Bears at Milwaukee.

   Aug. 23—At San Francisco.

   Aug. 29—Philadelphia at Portland, Ore.

   Sept. 5—New York at Bangor, Maine.

   Sept. 12—Washington at Winston-Salem, N.C.

   Sept. 20—Pittsburgh at Minneapolis.

LANDSMANN
Printing Office
226 Pine Street · Green Bay
Phone HEmlock 2-0221

LEAGUE

   Sept. 27—Chicago Bears at Green Bay.

   Oct. 4—Detroit at Green Bay.

   Oct. 11—San Francisco at Green Bay.

   Oct. 18—Los Angeles at Milwaukee.

   Oct. 25—At Baltimore.

   Nov. 1—At New York.

   Nov. 8—At Chicago Bears.

   Nov. 15—Baltimore at Milwaukee.

   Nov. 22—Washington at Green Bay.

   Nov. 26—At Detroit.

   Dec. 6—At Los Angeles.

   Dec. 13—At San Francisco.

PACKERS 1936 SCHEDULE

SEPT. 6—GREEN BAY WITH............	
	NON-LEAGUE CLUB_____
SEPT. 13—CHICAGO CARDS AT........	
	GREEN BAY_____
SEPT. 20—CHICAGO BEARS AT	
	GREEN BAY_____
SEPT. 27—OPEN	
OCT. 4—CHI. CARDS VS GREEN BAY_____	
	AT MILWAUKEE_____
OCT. 11—BOSTON AT..................	
	GREEN BAY_____
OCT. 18—DETROIT AT	
	GREEN BAY_____
OCT. 25—PITTSBURGH AT............	
	MILWAUKEE_____
NOV. 1—GREEN BAY AT	
	CHICAGO BEARS_____
NOV. 8—GREEN BAY AT	
	BOSTON_____
NOV. 15—GREEN BAY AT	
	BROOKLYN_____
NOV. 22—GREEN BAY AT	
	NEW YORK_____
NOV. 29—GREEN BAY AT	
	DETROIT_____
DEC. 6—GREEN BAY AT	
	CHICAGO CARDS_____

STIEFEL'S
"The Quality Store"

KUPPENHEIMER GOOD CLOTHES

1936 pocket schedule, back, Stiefel's Clothing, championship year ($25-$45).

1959 folding pocket schedule, inside, Lombardi's first year, Landsmann Printing ($10-$20).

1959 folding pocket schedule, outside, Lombardi's first year, Landsmann Printing ($10-$20).

BACK THE PACKERS

We Have

Since "1919"

LANDSMANN PRINTING

PACKERS 1959

N.F.L.

SCHEDULE

1965 pocket schedule, front, Landsmann Printing ($5-$15).

Select Your "PRINTER"
And (Stick) To Him.

226 PINE ST. — PH. 432-0221

Green Bay, Wisconsin

1965
GREEN BAY PACKER
SCHEDULE

Sept. 19—Green Bay at Pittsburgh
Sept. 26—Colts at Milwaukee
Oct. 3—Chicago at Green Bay
Oct. 10—San Fran. at Green Bay
Oct. 17—Green Bay at Detroit
Oct. 24—Dallas at Milwaukee
Oct. 31—Green Bay at Chicago
Nov. 7—Detroit at Green Bay
Nov. 14—Los Angeles at Milw.
Nov. 21—Green Bay at Minnesota
Nov. 28—Green Bay at L.A.
Dec. 5—Minnesota at Green Bay
Dec. 12—Green Bay at Baltimore
Dec. 19—Green Bay at San Fran.

Landsmann Printing Office

1965 pocket schedule, back, Landsmann Printing ($5-$15).

1968 Packer Schedule
Pre-Season

Fri., Aug. 2—College All-Stars at Chicago, 8 p.m.
Sat., Aug. 10—New York, 8 p.m.
Mon., Aug. 19—Chicago at Milwaukee, 8 p.m.
Sat., Aug. 24—At Dallas, 8:30 p.m.
Sat., Aug. 31—Steelers at Milwaukee, 8 p.m.
Sat., Sept. 7—At Cleveland, 9 p.m.

Regular Season

Sun., Sept. 15—Philadelphia, 1 p.m.
Sun., Sept. 22—Minnesota at Milwaukee, 1 p.m.
Sun., Sept. 29—Detroit, 1 p.m.
Sun., Oct. 6—At Atlanta, 1:30 p.m.
Sun., Oct. 13—Los Angeles at Milwaukee, 1 p.m.
Sun., Oct. 20—At Detroit, 1:15 p.m.
Mon., Oct. 28—At Dallas, 8:30 p.m.
Sun., Nov. 3—Chicago, 1 p.m.
Sun., Nov. 10—At Minnesota, 1:30 p.m.
Sun., Nov. 17—New Orleans at Milwaukee, 1 p.m.
Sun., Nov. 24—At Washington, 1:15 p.m.
Sun., Dec. 1—At San Francisco, 1 p.m.
Sat., Dec. 7—Baltimore, 1 p.m.
Sun., Dec. 15—At Chicago, 1 p.m.

1968 pocket schedule, back, Landsmann Printing ($5-$15).

1963-68 ruler schedules, Lombardi pictured on each ($15-$30 each).

1970s token schedules, aluminum ($5-$15 each).

192

Chapter 32

Scrapbooks

Scrapbooks can contain very interesting and valuable items. Ticket stubs, schedules, photographs, programs, postcards, newspaper clippings, Christmas cards and autographs all adorn the pages of old scrapbooks. Most items in scrapbooks were secured with glue or tape, causing items to have damage on the back. Newspaper clippings are among the most common and least valuable items in scrapbooks. Scrapbooks from the 1920s and 1930s are scarce and quite valuable. Scrapbooks from Championships and Super Bowl games can contain items worth several hundred dollars! Condition is important when estimating a scrapbook's price. Scrapbook values fall into two categories. First is the newspaper clippings that have less value. Second is the scrapbook that contain photos, autographs, tickets, schedules and many other items that can drastically increase its value.

Year	*Clippings Only*		*Miscellaneous Items*	
1920s	25.00	75.00	50.00	200.00+
1930s	20.00	50.00	40.00	150.00+
1940s	15.00	50.00	35.00	125.00+
1950s	10.00	35.00	25.00	100.00
1960s	10.00	50.00	20.00	100.00+
1970s	5.00	20.00	10.00	35.00
1980s	5.00	20.00	10.00	35.00
1990s	5.00	20.00	10.00	25.00

Most Career Opponent Fumbles Recovered

1. Willie Davis, 21 fumbles
2. Ray Nitschke, 20
3. Johnnie Gray, 20

Chapter 33

Stadium Memorabilia

Items that were part of the old city stadium or Lambeau Field are prized by collectors. Banners, flags, signs, goal posts, seats, flag poles, carpeting and other stadium items are gaining in popularity and value. When the old City Stadium was torn down in the early 1960s, wooden seats were cut up and sold as souvenirs. Pieces of goal posts have been a popular collectible since the 1960s. Any of the signs from tickets, parking, gates or entrances are valuable. The locker room carpeting with the Packers "G" has become difficult to obtain because it is not sold to the public. Stadium Flags and banners can range from a few dollars to more than $1,000, depending on age, condition and rarity. Whenever purchasing stadium items, try to get as much history and documentation on an item as possible. Condition, age, rarity, visual appeal and the history of an item all are important factors when assessing an item's value.

Item		*Price Range*
Frozen Tundra, with box and certificate	15.00	45.00
Piece of Old City Stadium, with box and photo	20.00	45.00
Pieces of goal post, depending on size	25.00	250.00+
Locker room carpeting, with "G"	15.00	50.00
Flags and banners	150.00	1,000.00+

Locker room nameplate, 1980-81, cardboard ($15-$25).

From left—piece of goal post mounted on plaque ($295); small piece of stadium with original decal ($20-$45); Frozen Tundra, with box and certificate ($15-$45).

Locker room carpeting, with "G" ($25).

Locker room nameplate, 1993-95, cardboard ($15-$25).

Chapter 34

Statues and Figures

Kenner Starting Lineup figures were introduced in 1988. Since then, just a handful of Packers have been featured on them. The key Packers Starting Lineup figures is the 1994 Brett Favre, which sells for more than $100. While the Packers figures from 1988 feature no big stars, they are quite valuable, as few were produced. Also included in this price list are some of the more popular players who were or are with the Packers, but who had figures made for them when they were with other clubs. The prices are for figures in their original packages.

Hartland Plastics (a Wisconsin-based company) made two generic statues for each NFL team in the 1960s—a running back and a lineman. These statues are tough to find.

Hartland

Statue	Price Range	
Green Bay running back	225.00	275.00
Green Bay lineman	200.00	250.00

Kenner Starting Lineup

Year	Player	Value
1988	Ken Davis	80.00
1988	Phillip Epps	35.00
1988	Brent Fullwood	40.00
1988	Mark Lee	45.00
1988	Reggie White (with Eagles)	100.00
1988	Randy Wright	50.00
1989	Keith Jackson (with Eagles)	60.00
1989	Sean Jones (with Oilers)	45.00
1989	James Lofton (with Raiders)	75.00
1989	Reggie White (with Eagles)	50.00
1990	Keith Jackson (with Eagles)	15.00
1990	Don Majkowski	15.00

1990	Reggie White (with Eagles)	35.00
1991	Don Majkowski	10.00
1991	Andre Rison (with Falcons)	22.50
1992	Seth Joyner (with Eagles)	11.00
1993	Sterling Sharpe	20.00
1994	Brett Favre	120.00
1994	Reggie White	20.00
1995	Brett Favre	45.00
1996	Steve Bono (with Chiefs)	10.00
1996	Robert Brooks	20.00
1996	Mark Brunell (with Jaguars)	35.00
1996	Brett Favre	45.00
1996	Bryce Paup (with Bills)	11.00
1996	Reggie White	16.00
1997	Mark Chmura	20.00
1997	Brett Favre	30.00
1997	Reggie White	12.00
1997	Brett Favre & Bart Starr/Classic Doubles	40.00

1960s Hartland statues, plastic, from left—Green Bay running back ($225-$275); Green Bay lineman ($200-$250).

Chapter 35

Stickers

Bumper stickers were very popular in the 1950s through the 1970s. Chrome bumpers allowed stickers to be applied and removed easily. many of the modern cars have painted bumpers that are damaged when removing bumper stickers. A large variety of sayings, subjects and shapes make collecting bumper stickers both challenging and fun. Players photos, schedules, jingles and special events all adorned bumper stickers. Prices range from a few dollars up to almost $100. Window decals differ from bumper stickers in that they are made to stick to the inside of glass instead of having an adhesive back like bumper stickers. Stadium dedication, Championship and Super Bowl stickers have risen in value during recent years. Because bumper stickers and window decals are not reusable, they are getting harder to find. Condition is important in determining a sticker's value. Tears, fading and holes all detract from value.

Year	*Price Range*	
1930s (rare)	150.00	175.00+
1940s	50.00	125.00
1950s	35.00	100.00
1960s	15.00	75.00
1970s	5.00	25.00
1980s	3.00	15.00
1990s	2.00	10.00

1962 "World Champion" sticker, 3" x 14" ($35-$75).

1965 window decal, schedule on back ($10-$30).

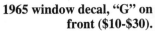

1965 window decal, "G" on front ($10-$30).

1960s "World Champs" sticker, #15 throwing pass, ($20-$40).

Super Bowl II, cloth iron-on, green and white ($10-$25).

1960s "World's Champion" sticker, green and gold, 4" ($15-$30).

1970s "The Pack Has A Guiding Starr" sticker ($8-$20).

1960s reflective sticker, 3" ($5-$15).

1960s/70s sticker, single-bar face mask ($3-$7).

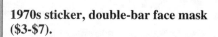

1970s sticker, double-bar face mask ($3-$7).

1993 75th Anniversary sticker, black ($3-$7).

1969 "We'll Win With Bengston" sticker, 50-year anniversary ($10-$25).

Early 1970s, "The 'Pack' Will Be Back" sticker ($6-$15).

1971 "We Love Ray" (Nitsch-ke) sticker, green and gold ($10-$30).

1960s "Go Pack Go!" sticker ($10-$25).

1970s Packers Hall of Fame sticker, green and gold ($8-$20).

STICK WITH STARR

1980s "Stick With Starr" sticker, green and gold ($5-$10).

1973 schedule sticker, bank give-away ($5-$10).

1973
GREEN BAY
PACKERS
League Games

Sep. 17 JETS at Mke.	Nov. 4 BEARS at G. B.
Sep. 23 LIONS at G. B.	Nov. 11 CARDINALS at G.B.
Sep. 30 VIKINGS at Minn.	Nov. 18 PATRIOTS at N. E.
Oct. 7 GIANTS at N. Y.	Nov. 26 49ERS at S. F.
Oct. 14 CHIEFS at Mke.	Dec. 2 SAINTS at Mke.
Oct. 21 RAMS at L. A.	Dec. 8 VIKINGS at G. B.
Oct. 28 LIONS at Det.	Dec. 16 BEARS at Chgo.

THE PACK WILL FLY HIGH WITH LINDY

1988-91 "The Pack Will Fly High With Lindy" sticker ($5-$10).

Chapter 36

Tickets

The 1920s Packers tickets were small plain tickets with numbers on both ends. They are very rare and command premium prices. Tickets from the 1930s are also difficult to find and valuable. The 1940s tickets were a different color each game and they are much easier to find then 1920s and 1930s tickets. The 1950s tickets have some value, but they are not as prized or valuable as the 1920s through the 1940s tickets. The 1960s tickets provide both championship and Super Bowl tickets. Tickets from the Lombardi era (1959 to 1967) are very collectible. Tickets from Championship years (1929, 1930, 1931, 1936, 1939, 1944, 1961, 1962, 1965, 1966, 1967, 1996) have more value than tickets from non-championship years. Tickets from special games such as Championships, Playoff games, stadium dedication, a record set, coaches' or players' first or last games, etc., can increase the value significantly.

Condition is an important factor in assessing value. Creases, tears, stains, holes, fading and writing all detract from a ticket's value. Full tickets are much more valuable than torn tickets. The smaller torn tickets are referred to as a stub. The size of the stub and which half of the ticket was saved both affect the value.

Regular Season	Ticket Stub		Full Ticket	
1920s	50.00	150.00	n/a	
1930s	30.00	100.00	45.00	100.00+
1940s	15.00	50.00	35.00	75.00
1950s	10.00	25.00	20.00	50.00
1960s	5.00	15.00	15.00	35.00
1970s	3.00	10.00	8.00	25.00
1980s	3.00	10.00	6.00	20.00
1990s	5.00	20.00	10.00	30.00

Championship Game	Ticket Stub		Full Ticket	
1930s	100.00	250.00	200.00	600.00+
1940s	75.00	200.00	150.00	500.00+
1960s	75.00	200.00	150.00	600.00+
1990s	35.00	100.00	75.00	200.00

Tickets, from left—Super Bowl I, full, 1/15/67; Super Bowl II, full, 1/14/68 ($350-$1,000 each).

1962-66 ticket stubs, various games ($5-$15 each).

1949 ticket stubs, vs. Rams, 10/2/49 ($10-$25 each).

1965 playoff ticket stubs vs. Colts, (phantom field goal game), 12/26/65 ($15-$35 each).

1961-65 ticket stubs, various games ($5-$15 each).

1960 NFL Championship, ticket stub, at Philadelphia, large half, 12/26/60 ($50-$95).

1965 NFL Championship ticket stub, vs. Cleveland Browns, 1/2/66 ($35-$75).

1966 NFL Championship ticket stub, at Dallas, winner plays in Super Bowl I, 1/1/67 ($50-$95).

1961 NFL Championship, full ticket, vs. NY Giants, 12/31/61 ($150-$350).

1952 and 1956 ticket stubs ($10-$20 each).

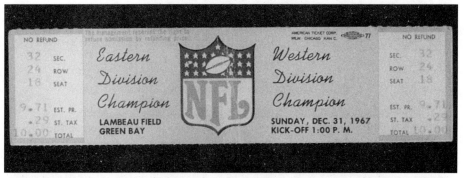

1967 NFL Championship, full ticket, vs. Dallas, Ice Bowl, 12/31/67 ($100-$300+)

Chapter 37

Trading Cards

This section contains the top trading cards from Packers Hall of Famers; other popular Packers non-Hall of Famers (Max McGee, Jerry Kramer, etc.); and current stars (Brett Favre, Reggie White, etc.). With so many more card companies making cards over the last 10 years, a player like Favre has several hundred different cards. Only those cards that carry a premium are included in this list. Also, many of the old-time Packers have had cards released after their playing days were over. Most of these cards are inexpensive and not listed here. Some players, especially those who played in the 1920s through the 1950s, have very few cards available.

Trading card collectors are very condition conscious. Cards that are off-center, creased, have writing on them or have dings or nicks on the sides and corners are factors that detract from value. The prices below are for cards in Near Mint condition (on pre-1980 cards) and Mint condition (for cards 1980 to the present).

Herb Adderley (HOF, 1981)

Card	No.	Value
1961 Packers Lake to Lake	30	12.00
1964 Philadelphia	71	30.00
1964 Wheaties Stamps	1	6.00

1968 Topps, #131

1965 Philadelphia	72	8.00
1966 Philadelphia	80	5.00
1967 Philadelphia	74	4.50
1967 Williams Portraits	193	12.00
1968 Topps	131	3.00
1969 Topps	255	4.00
1969 Topps Four In Ones	36	2.00
1971 Cowboys Team Issue	1	5.00
1972 Cowboys Team Issue	1	4.00
1972 NFLPA Wonderful World Stamps	91	3.00
1972 Topps	66	2.50
1973 Topps	243	2.25

Donny Anderson

Card	*No.*	*Value*
1967 Williams Portraits	195	8.00
1968 Topps	209	4.00
1969 Packers Tasco Prints	1	10.00
1969 Topps	237	1.15
1969 Topps Four In Ones	21	4.00
1970 Clark Oil/Volpe Green Bay Packers	2	4.50
1970 Clark Volpe	32	6.00
1971 Kellogg's	51	5.00
1971 Mattel Mini-Records	1	4.00

1973 Topps, #265

John Anderson

Card	No.	Value
1977 Michigan	1	1.25
1983 Packers Police	59	1.25
1983 Topps	75	1.00
1987 Acc Fact Pack Green Bay Packers	1	6.00

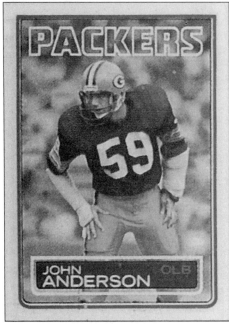

1983 Topps, #75

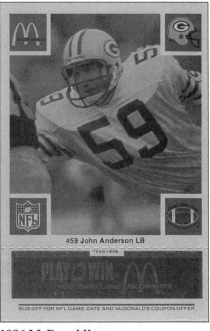

1986 McDonald's

Edgar Bennett

Card	No.	Value
1992 Action Packed Rookies Update	36	3.00
1992 Fleer GameDay	498	4.00
1992 Pinnacle	323	2.00
1992 Pro Line Portraits Autographs	331	12.00
1992 Stadium Club	388	2.00

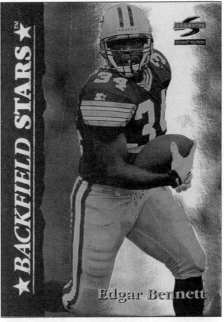

1996 Pro Line, #51

1995 Score Summit Edition, Backfield Stars, #15

1995 Score Summit Edition, Backfield Stars, #15

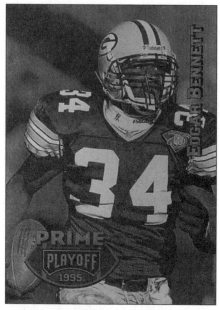

1995 Prime Playoff, #105

1995 Topps Stadium Club, #178

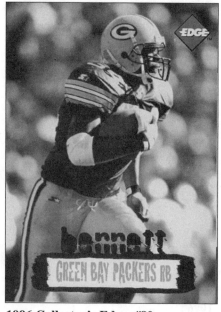

1996 Collector's Edge, #80

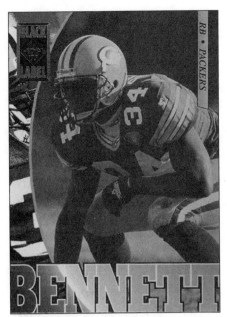

1995 Collector's Edge Black Label, #70

1995 Action Packed, #74

1995 Bowman, #56

1996 Pinnacle Summit, #78

John Brockington

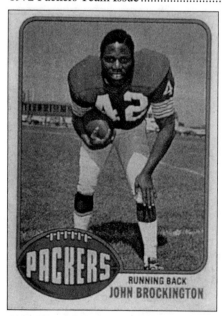

1976 Topps, #345

1974 Topps, #400

1972 Topps, #273

1972 Topps	273	20.00
1972 Topps	85	4.00
1973 Topps	470	1.00
1974 Nabisco Sugar Daddy	8	2.50
1974 Packers Team Issue	1	5.00
1974 Topps (with O.J. Simpson)	328	5.00
1974 Topps	400	.75
1975 Nabisco Sugar Daddy	8	2.50
1976 Crane Discs	5	.25
1976 Pepsi Discs	9	.75
1977 Topps Holsum Packers/Vikings	2	2.00

Robert Brooks

Card	*No.*	*Value*
1992 Fleer	56	6.00
1992 All-World	58	2.00
1992 Collector's Edge	230	2.00
1992 Fleer GameDay	413	2.00
1992 SkyBox Impact	333	2.00

1995 Flair, #73

1995 Topps Stadium Club, #114

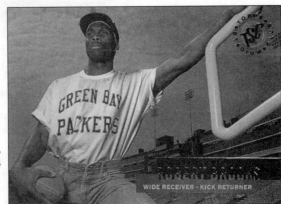

1995 Score Summit Edition, silver, #195

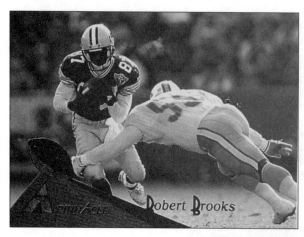

1994 Pinnacle, #261

1996 SkyBox Premium, #240

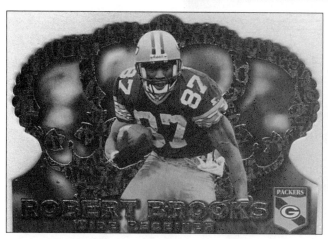

1997 Pacific Crown, #CR-115

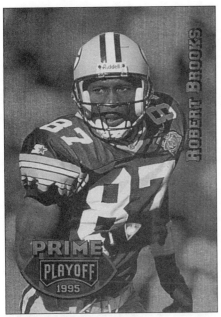

1995 Prime Playoff, #172

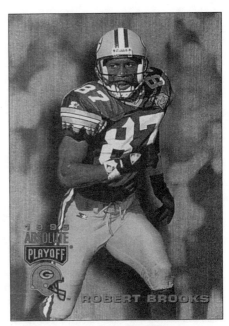

1995 Absolute Playoff, #172

1995 Action Packed, #10

1994 Fleer Ultra, #390

1996 SP, #36

1995 Fleer Ultra, #110

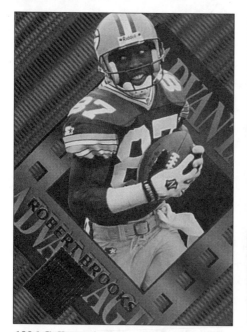

1996 Collector's Edge Advantage, #95

1996 Topps Stadium Club, #302

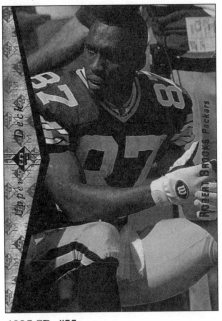

1995 SP, #55

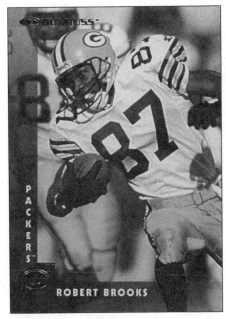

1997 Donruss, #34

1996 Playoff Prime Surprise	PS11	25.00
1996 Playoff Prime X's and O's	171	4.00
1996 Playoff Trophy Contenders Mini Back-to-Backs	15	60.00
1996 Playoff Trophy Contenders Playoff Zone	25	10.00
1996 Pro Line DC I Road to the Super Bowl	14	8.00
1996 SkyBox Impact Rookies Draft Board	10	4.00
1996 Stadium Club Fusion	5B	4.00
1996 Upper Deck Silver Helmet Cards	NC5	6.00
1996 Zenith Artist's Proofs	79	20.00
1996 Zenith Artist's Proofs	142	5.00
1997 Collector's Edge Excalibur Marauders	23	3.00
1997 Fleer Goudey Heads Up	4	3.00
1997 Fleer Goudey Pigskin 2000	4	10.00
1997 Pacific Dynagon Tandems	10	20.00
1997 Playoff Absolute Leather Quads	LQ9	60.00
1997 Playoff Absolute Pennants	103	10.00
1997 Playoff Absolute Reflex	4	30.00
1997 Playoff 1st & 10 Hot Pursuit	4	20.00

LeRoy Butler

Card	No.	Value
1990 Score	619	.50
1991 Bowman	175	.50
1991 Pacific	151	.50
1991 Pinnacle	217	.65
1991 Pro Set	507	.50
1991 Score	456	.50
1991 Stadium Club	248	.75
1991 Topps	450	.50
1992 Pro Line Portraits Autographs	309	3.00
1993 McDonald's GameDay	28	2.00
1993 Packers Police	10	.75
1994 Action Packed All-Madden 24k Gold	39	20.00
1994 Packers Police	19	.50
1994 Stadium Club First Day Cards	63	2.00
1995 Finest Refractors	275	3.00

1994 Fleer Ultra, #391

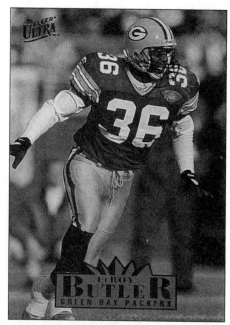

1995 Fleer Ultra, #111

1994 Pinnacle, #223

	No.	Value
1995 Topps Florida Hot Bed	FH14	1.00
1997 Fleer All-Pro	15	2.00
1997 Playoff Absolute Reflex	103	30.00

Tony Canadeo (HOF, 1974)

Card	No.	Value
1948 Exhibit Football	5	12.00
1948-52 Exhibit W468 Football	5	15.00
1950 Bowman	9	55.00
1951 Bowman	90	30.00
1975 Fleer Hall of Fame	76	.35
1977 Touchdown Club	49	1.25
1989 Goal Line Hall of Fame	65	2.00
1993 Packers Archives Postcards	19	.75

Willie Davis (HOF, 1980)

Card	No.	Value
1960 Kahn's	6	65.00
1961 Packers Lake to Lake	3	50.00
1964 Philadelphia	72	30.00

	No.	Value
1964 Wheaties Stamps	16	6.00
1965 Philadelphia	73	8.00
1966 Philadelphia	83	5.00
1967 Philadelphia	76	4.50
1967 Williams Portraits	204	15.00
1969 Glendale Stamps	125	1.50
1989 Goal Line Hall of Fame	153	3.00
1990 Packers 25th Anniversary	29	.75
1991 Action Packed Whizzer White Greats	2	4.00
1991 Packers Super Bowl I	36	.75
1992 Packers Hall of Fame	106	.50

Lynn Dickey

Card	No.	Value
1971 Oilers Team Issue	9	4.00
1973 Oilers Team Issue	5	3.00
1974 Topps	252	3.00
1975 Topps	243	.75
1977 Topps	376	.50
1977 Topps Holsum Packers/Vikings	1	3.00
1983 Packers Police	12	1.50
1984 Packers Police	8	1.00

1985 Topps

1983 Topps, #77

1986 McDonald's

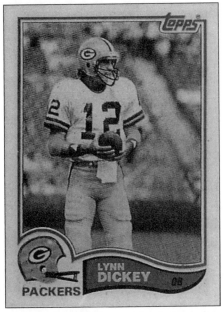

1982 Topps, #357

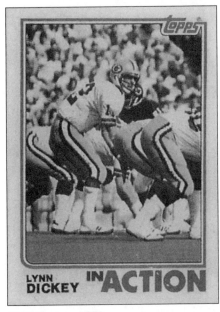

1982 Topps, #358

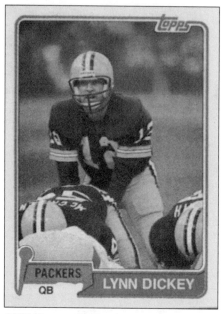

1982 Topps, #357

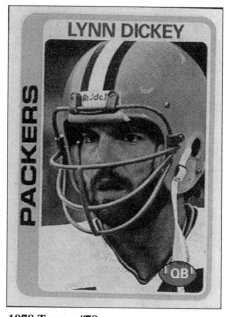

1978 Topps, #78

1974 Topps, #252

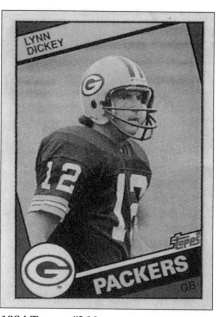

1984 Topps, #266

Card	No.	Value
1984 7-11 Discs	11W	.75
1985 Packers Police	25	.75
1986 McDonald's Green Bay Packers	12	.50
1986 Packers Police	12	.60
1993 Metallic Images QB Legends	4	1.50

Boyd Dowler

Card	*No.*	*Value*
1961 Fleer	92	8.00
1961 Packers Lake to Lake	24	30.00
1961 Topps	43	5.00
1962 Post Cereal	2	3.50
1962 Topps	71	3.50
1963 Topps	88	2.00
1965 Philadelphia	74	1.50
1966 Packers Mobil Posters	5	12.00
1966 Philadelphia	84	1.50
1967 Williams Portraits	205	8.00
1968 Topps	105	1.00
1969 Packers Tasco Prints	2	10.00
1969 Topps	33	1.00
1991 Packers Super Bowl I	37	.50
1992 Packers Hall of Fame	78	.30

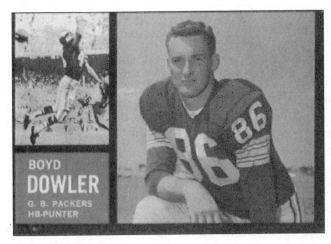

1962 Topps, #71

229

Brett Favre

Card	No.	Value
1991 Action Packed Rookie Update	21	8.00
1991 Pacific	551	3.00
1991 Pro Set	762	3.00
1991 Score	611	3.00
1991 Stadium Club	94	70.00
1991 Ultra	283	3.50
1991 Ultra Update	1	25.00
1991 Upper Deck	13	4.00
1992 Packers Police	5	6.00
1992 Pinnacle	303	5.00
1992 Pinnacle Team 2000	23	5.00
1992 Stadium Club	683	90.00
1992 Upper Deck Coach's Report	5	10.00
1992 Wild Card Stat Smashers	SS23	10.00
1993 Action Packed Monday Night Football Mint	38	175.00
1993 Action Packed Quarterback Club	5	6.00
1993 Action Packed Quarterback Club Braille	5	10.00
1993 Action Packed 24k Gold	5	125.00
1993 Bowman	335	8.00
1993 Fleer Team Leaders	1	20.00
1993-95 Highland Mint Topps	7	100.00
1993 Pacific Gold Prisms	5	30.00
1993 Pacific Prisms	31	12.00
1993 Pacific Silver Prism Inserts	5	15.00
1993 Packers Police	9	4.00
1993 Pinnacle Samples	1	6.00
1993 Pinnacle Team 2001	7	8.00
1993 Playoff Brett Favre, each	1-5	10.00
1993 Playoff Headliners Redemption	H1	14.00
1993 Pro Line Live Autographs	88	175.00
1993 Pro Line Live LPs	LP10	8.00
1993 Pro Line Portraits Autographs	486	250.00
1993 Score Ore-Ida QB Club	9	6.00

1997 Pacific Player of the Week, #18

1996 Upper Deck, #131

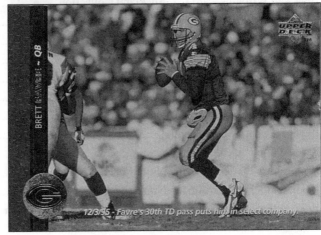

1995 Action Packed Rookies & Stars 24k Gold Team	2	55.00
1995 Action Packed Rookies & Stars Closing Seconds	6	17.00
1995 Action Packed 24k Gold	9G	90.00
1995 Bowman's Best	V43	8.00
1995 Bowman's Best Refractors	V43	100.00
1995 Collector's Edge EdgeTech	21	12.00
1995 Collector's Edge Excalibur 22k Gold	33	100.00
1995 Collector's Edge 12th Man Redemption	4	8.00
1995 Finest	56	12.00
1995 Finest Refractors	56	150.00
1995 Flair	75	6.00
1995 Flair Hot Numbers	6	14.00
1995-96 Highland Mint Bronze Medallions	3	14.00
1995 Images Limited/Live Icons	I8	25.00
1995 Images Limited/Live Focused	F15	20.00
1995 Images Limited/Live Die-Cuts	DC21	50.00
1995 Metal Gold Blasters	6	12.00
1995 Metal Silver Flashers	16	8.00
1995 Pacific Crown Royale Pride of the NFL	PN12	35.00
1995 Pacific Crown Royale	139	10.00
1995 Pacific Gems of the Crown	12	16.00
1995 Pacific Gridiron	38	8.00
1995 Pacific Prisms	142	12.00
1995 Pacific Triple Folder Big Guns	6	10.00
1995 Pinnacle Artist's Proof	26	90.00
1995 Pinnacle Black 'N Blue	25	50.00
1995 Pinnacle Club Collection Arms Race	5	10.00
1995 Pinnacle Showcase	10	14.00
1995 Pinnacle Team Pinnacle	7	50.00
1995 Playoff Absolute Die Cut Helmets	6	70.00
1995 Playoff Absolute Quad Series	2	225.00
1995 Playoff Contenders Back-to-Back	3	125.00
1995 Playoff Contenders Hog Heaven	10	150.00
1995 Playoff Prime Fantasy Team	6	40.00
1995 Playoff Prime Minis	35	50.00
1995 Pro Line Field Generals	9	50.00

1995 Pro Line Game Breakers	GB9	20.00
1995 Pro Line Impact	8	18.00
1995 Pro Line MVP Redemption	14	30.00
1995 Score Offense Inc.	8	12.00
1995 Score Pass Time	7	30.00
1995 Select Certified	50	7.00
1995 Select Certified Gold Team	9	70.00
1995 Select Certified Mirror Certified Mirror Golds	50	60.00
1995 Select Certified Select Few	6	60.00
1995 SkyBox Impact	M1	25.00
1995 SkyBox Impact Countdown	9	15.00
1995 SkyBox Paydirt	PD10	8.00
1995 Sp	56	6.00
1995 Sp All-Pros	4	8.00
1995 Sp Championship Playoff Showcase	6	25.00
1995 Sp Holoview Die-Cuts	36	125.00
1995 Sp Holoviews	36	20.00
1995 Sportflix Man 2 Man	11	15.00
1995 Stadium Club Ground Attack	2	15.00
1995 Stadium Club Nemeses	4	25.00
1995 Stadium Club Nightmares	28	25.00
1995 Summit Team Summit	10	80.00
1995 Topps Finest Inserts	-	16.00
1995-96 Topps Finest Pro Bowl Jumbos	5	14.00
1995-96 Topps Finest Pro Bowl Jumbos Refractors	5	275.00
1995 Topps Yesteryear	15	20.00
1995 Topps 100/300 Boosters	34	20.00
1995 Ultra Magna Force	16	20.00
1995 Ultra Rising Stars	6	25.00
1995 Ultra Ultrabilities	9	10.00
1995 Upper Deck Retail Predictor	6	12.00
1995 Zenith	62	10.00
1995 Zenith Second Season	1	20.00
1995 Zenith Z-Team	9	70.00
1996 Action Packed Artist's Proof	18	125.00
1996 Action Packed Longest Yard	1	35.00

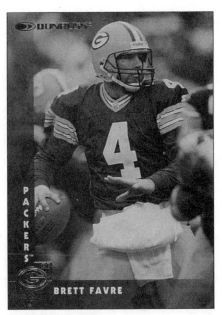

1997 Donruss, #2

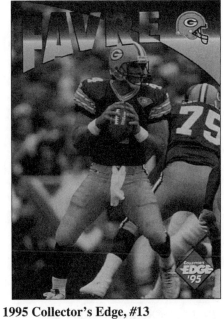

1995 Collector's Edge, #13

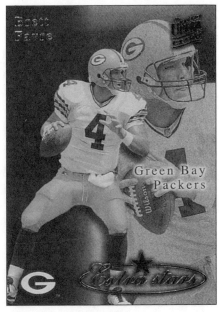

1995 Fleer Ultra, #490

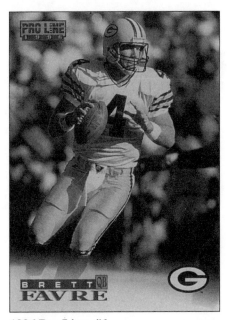

1996 Pro Line, #6

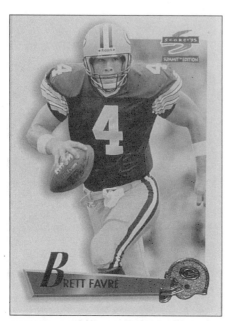

1995 Score Summit Edition, #32

1995 Action Packed, #60

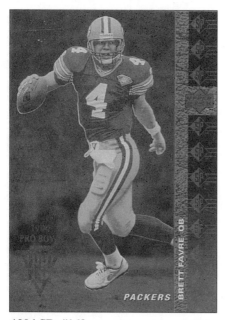

1994 SP, #163

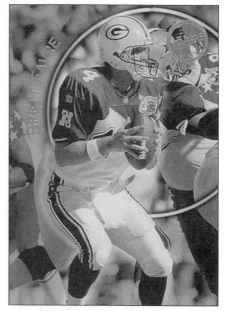

1996 Topps Members Only, #1

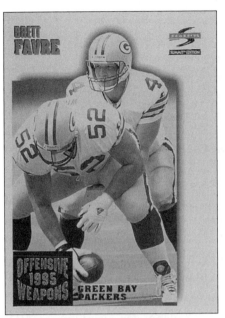

1995 Score Summit Edition, #193

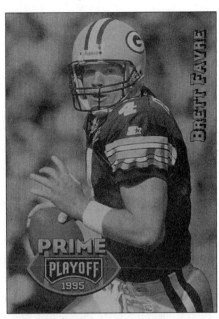

1995 Prime Playoff, #35

1996 Pro Line III, #41

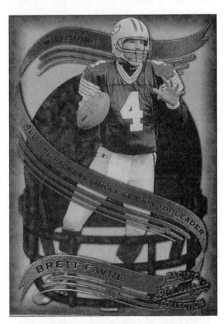

1997 Pacific Philadelphia Collection, #7

1996 Action Packed Sculptor's Proof	4	150.00
1996 Action Packed The Longest Yard	1	40.00
1996 Action Packed 24kt Gold	1	80.00
1996 Bowman's Best	70	8.00
1996 Bowman's Best Best Cuts	5	40.00
1996 Bowman's Best Mirror Images	2a	40.00
1996 Classic NFL Experience Sculpted	S9	20.00
1996 Classic NFL Experience Super Bowl Die Cut Promos	9C	12.00
1996 Classic NFL Experience Super Bowl Die Cut Contest, each	9a or 9b	20.00
1996 Collector's Choice Crash The Game	6	6.00
1996 Collector's Edge Advantage Edge Video	1	35.00
1996 Collector's Edge Advantage Game Ball	3	150.00
1996 Collector's Edge President's Reserve Air Force One	1	30.00
1996 Collector's Edge President's Reserve Pro Bowl '96	3	16.00
1996 Collector's Edge President's Reserve TimeWarp	6	100.00
1996 Collector's Edge President's Reserve Running Mates	13	90.00
1996 Collector's Edge President's Reserve	70	6.00
1996 Collector's Edge Quantum	10	40.00
1996 Collector's Edge Ripped	6	12.00
1996 Donruss Elite	9	40.00
1996 Donruss Hit List	5	25.00
1996 Donruss Stop Action	3	50.00
1996 Donruss What If?	6	40.00
1996 Donruss Will to Win	2	30.00
1996 Finest	4	25.00
1996 Finest	132	85.00
1996 Finest Refractors	4	200.00
1996 Finest Refractors	132	625.00
1996 Fleer Statistically Speaking	4	20.00
1996 Laser View	7	10.00
1996 Laser View Inscriptions	-	125.00
1996 Leaf Gold Leaf Stars	11	80.00
1996 Leaf Shirt Off My Back	10	60.00
1996 Leaf Statistical Standouts	15	80.00
1996 Metal Goldflingers	5	14.00

1996 Playoff Absolute Xtreme Team	5	40.00
1996 Playoff Absolute/Prime Metal XL	4	80.00
1996 Playoff Contenders Air Command	2	90.00
1996 Playoff Contenders Leather	1	100.00
1996 Playoff Contenders Leather Accents	1	600.00
1996 Playoff Contenders Open Field	1	20.00
1996 Playoff Contenders Pennants	1	90.00
1996 Playoff Illusions	100	10.00
1996 Playoff Illusions Optical Illusions	1	150.00
1996 Playoff Illusions Spectralusion Elite	100	20.00
1996 Playoff Prime Boss Hogs	14	100.00
1996 Playoff Prime Playoff Honors	PH3	350.00
1996 Playoff Prime Surprise	PS2	200.00
1996 Playoff Prime X's and O's	1	50.00
1996 Playoff Trophy Contenders Playoff Zone	4	50.00
1996 Playoff Trophy Contenders Mini Back-to-Backs	12	90.00
1996 Pro Line Cels	C13	50.00
1996 Pro Line DC I	41	6.00
1996 Pro Line DC I All-Pros	AP8	80.00
1996 Pro Line DC I Road to the Super Bowl	13	45.00
1996 Pro Line I Intense $3 Phone Cards	8	12.00
1996 Pro Line Memorabilia Producers	6	10.00
1996 Pro Line Memorabilia Stretch Drive	12	18.00
1996 Pro Line Rivalries	R9	20.00
1996 Score Artist's Proofs	119	35.00
1996 Score Artist's Proofs	245	20.00
1996 Score Artist's Proofs	273	15.00
1996 Score Board NFL Lasers Laser Images	I11	30.00
1996 Score Board NFL Lasers Sunday's Heroes	S12	50.00
1996 Score Dream Team	6	30.00
1996 Score Footsteps	9	15.00
1996 Score In the Zone	1	30.00
1996 Score Numbers Game	3	12.00
1996 Score Settle the Score, Nos. 7, 19	each	35.00
1996 Score Settle the Score	21	20.00
1996 Select Artist's Proofs	10	70.00

1996 Select Artist's Proofs	182	35.00
1996 Select Certified Gold Team	11	60.00
1996 Select Certified Thumbs Up	7	60.00
1996 Select Four-Midable	5	20.00
1996 Select Prime Cut	7	70.00
1996 SkyBox Autographs	-	250.00
1996 SkyBox Brett Favre MVP, Nos. 1, 2, 3b	each	40.00
1996 SkyBox Brett Favre MVP, Nos. 3a, 4, 5	each	30.00
1996 SkyBox Brett Favre MVP	3c	60.00
1996 SkyBox Impact No Surrender	5	30.00
1996 SkyBox Impact Rookies Rookie Rewind	5	18.00
1996 SkyBox SkyMotion	17	15.00
1996 SkyBox SkyMotion Team Galaxy	2	50.00
1996 SkyBox Thunder and Lightning	7	40.00
1996 Sp Explosive	X4	250.00
1996 Sp Holoview	4	25.00
1996 Sp Spx Force	3	250.00
1996 Spx	17	15.00
1996 Stadium Club Dot Matrix	250	25.00
1996 Stadium Club Fusion	5A	30.00
1996 Stadium Club Laser Sites	1	25.00
1996 Stadium Club Photo Gallery	15	25.00
1996 Stadium Club Pro Bowl	1	30.00
1996 Summit Inspirations	5	30.00
1996 Summit Third and Long	6	80.00
1996 Summit Turf Team	2	50.00
1996 Topps Broadway's Reviews	4	7.00
1996 Topps Chrome 40th Anniversary	7	20.00
1996 Topps Gilt Edge Definitive Edge	2	8.00
1996 Topps Hobby Masters	1	25.00
1996 Topps Laser	80	6.00
1996 Topps Laser Stadium Stars	5	80.00
1996 Topps Turf Warriors	5	20.00
1996 Topps 40th Anniversary	7	10.00
1996 Ultra Mr. Momentum	6	15.00
1996 Ultra Pulsating	2	16.00

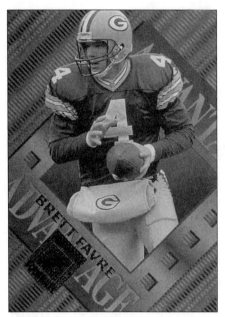

1996 Collector's Edge, #13

1996 Topps Stadium Club, #174

1996 Pinnacle, #40

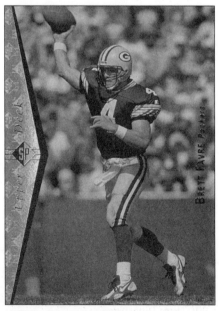

1995 Upper Deck, #56

1996 Ultra Sensations Creative Chaos, 19 different...................................each		10.00-18.00
1996 Upper Deck Hot Properties HT4		20.00
1996 Upper Deck Predictor.. PH3		50.00
1996 Upper Deck Pro Bowl PB2		20.00
1996 Upper Deck Proview 3		16.00
1996 Upper Deck Silver All-NFL..AN7		10.00
1996 Upper Deck Team Trio 41		6.00
1996 Upper Deck TV Cels.. PH3		125.00
1996 Zenith Artist's Proofs...21		125.00
1996 Zenith Artist's Proofs..144		60.00
1996 Zenith Noteworthy '95...7		14.00
1996 Zenith Z-Team 9		100.00
1997 Action Packed Crash Course...5		40.00
1997 Action Packed 24K Team 1		90.00
1997 Collector's Choice Turf Champions TC81		75.00
1997 Collector's Edge Excalibur Game Gear...1		100.00
1997 Collector's Edge Excalibur 22k Knights 3		25.00
1997 Collector's Edge Excalibur Marauders..3		25.00
1997 Collector's Edge Excalibur Over Lords...18		25.00
1997 Collector's Edge Excalibur Castle Cards.......................................18		25.00
1997 Collector's Edge Masters Super Bowl XXXI Game Ball................1		300.00
1997 Collector's Edge Masters Radical Rivals..2		25.00
1997 Collector's Edge Masters Night Games...6		20.00
1997 Collector's Edge Masters Playoff Game Ball 14		110.00
1997 Collector's Edge Masters Playoff Game Ball 18		120.00
1997 Donruss Elite...3		50.00
1997 Donruss Legends of the Fall 8		35.00
1997 Donruss Passing Grade 12		45.00
1997 E-X200 13		12.00
1997 E-X200 A Cut Above..2		120.00
1997 Finest...150		25.00
1997 Finest Refractors 150		150.00
1997 Fleer All-Pro 7		30.00
1997 Fleer Goudey Heads Up...8		30.00
1997 Fleer Goudey Tittle Says...9		30.00
1997 Fleer Thrill Seekers 5		90.00

1994 GameDay, #147

1996 Pinnacle Summit, #192

1997 Pro Line Gems Championship Ring	CR1	100.00
1997 Pro Line Gems Through the Years	TY2	25.00
1997 Pro Line Rivalries	R13	40.00
1997 Score Board NFL $25 Die-Cut Phone Cards	10	30.00
1997 Score Board NFL Experience Foundations	F22	15.00
1997 Score Franchise	3	35.00
1997 Score New Breed	18	12.00
1997 Score The Specialist	1	12.00
1997 SkyBox Impact Boss	10	6.00
1997 SkyBox Impact Rave Reviews	3	120.00
1997 Spx	43	12.00

Card	No.	Value
1997 Spx Holofame	4	90.00
1997 Stadium Club Aerial Assault	AA10	12.00
1997 Stadium Club Bowman's Best Previews	BBP6	25.00
1997 Topps Gallery	100	5.00
1997 Topps Gallery of Heroes	GH10	45.00
1997 Topps Gallery Critics Choice	C10	40.00
1997 Topps Gallery Peter Max	PM1	25.00
1997 Topps Gallery Photo Gallery	PG3	35.00
1997 Topps Hall Bound	HB10	25.00
1997 Topps High Octane	HO1	25.00
1997 Topps Mystery Finest	M20	25.00
1997 Topps Season's Best	4	16.00
1997 Topps Stars	1	6.00
1997 Topps Stars Pro Bowl Stars	PB1	80.00
1997 Ultra Blitzkrieg	6	15.00
1997 Ultra Starring Role	9	100.00
1997 Upper Deck Black Diamond Title Quest	7	350.00
1997 Upper Deck Black Diamond	154	50.00
1997 Upper Deck Game Jersey	GM4	600.00
1997 Upper Deck Game Jersey	GM5	600.00
1997 Upper Deck MVP	MP14	70.00
1997 Zenith V2	12	50.00
1997 Zenith Z-Team	11	80.00

Antonio Freeman

Card	*No.*	*Value*
1995 Bowman	217	3.00
1995 Bowman's Best	R90	6.00
1995 Bowman's Best Refractors	R90	40.00
1995 Pacific Crown Royale	73	7.00
1995 Pacific Prisms	205	8.00
1995 Sp Championship	18	3.00
1995 SR Draft Preview Signatures	31	10.00
1996 Playoff Absolute Promos	-	3.00
1996 Playoff Absolute Quad Series	11	15.00

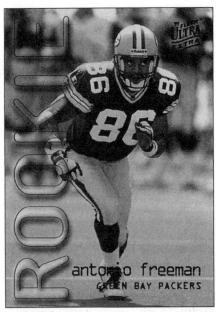

1995 Fleer Ultra, #433

1996 Playoff Illusions, #55

1996 Collector's Edge, #52

1996 Pinnacle, #98

248

Forrest Gregg (HOF, 1977)

Card	No.	Value
1960 Topps	56	28.00
1961 Fleer	94	8.50
1961 Packers Lake to Lake	27	7.50
1962 Post Cereal	4	4.00
1962 Salada Coins	21	15.00
1962 Topps	70	7.50
1963 Kahn's	25	25.00
1963 Topps	89	5.25
1964 Philadelphia	73	4.00
1964 Wheaties Stamps	27	5.00
1965 Philadelphia	75	4.00
1966 Philadelphia	85	4.00
1967 Philadelphia	77	4.00
1967 Williams Portraits	209	15.00
1984 Packers Police	2	2.00
1985-87 Packers Police	each	1.00-1.75
1989 Goal Line Hall of Fame	68	2.50
1990 Packers 25th Anniversary	25	.75
1992 Packers Hall of Fame	67	.50

1962 Topps, #70

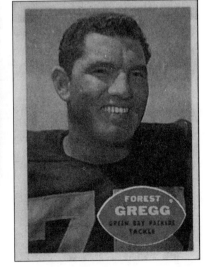

1960 Topps, #56

Arnie Herber (HOF, 1966)

Card	No.	Value
1933 Diamond Matchbooks Silver	39	20.00
1975 Fleer Hall of Fame	73	.35
1985-87 Football Immortals	52	.35
1989 Goal Line Hall of Fame	160	2.00
1992 Packers Hall of Fame	27	.30

Clarke Hinkle (HOF, 1964)

Card	No.	Value
1933 Diamond Matchbooks Silver	42	20.00
1935 National Chicle	24	200.00
1963 Stancraft Playing Cards	4S	2.00
1974 Fleer Hall of Fame	20	1.25
1975 Fleer Hall of Fame	10	.35
1977 Touchdown Club	30	1.00
1989 Goal Line Hall of Fame	14	2.50
1992 Packers Hall of Fame	23	.50

Paul Hornung (HOF, 1986)

Card	No.	Value
1957 Topps	151	400.00
1959 Topps	82	60.00
1960 Topps	54	35.00
1961 Fleer	90	45.00
1961 Packers Lake to Lake	10	15.00
1961 Topps	38	10.00
1961 Topps	40	28.00
1962 Post Booklets	2	25.00
1962 Post Cereal	6	14.00
1962 Salada Coins	12	25.00
1962 Topps	64	50.00
1962 Topps Bucks	5	18.00

1962 Topps, #64

1960 Topps, #54

Robert "Cal" Hubbard (HOF, 1963)

Card	No.	Value
1975 Fleer Hall of Fame	17	.35
1988 Swell Football Greats	56	.10

Don Hutson (HOF, 1963)

Card	No.	Value
1955 Topps All-Americans	97	200.00
1963 Stancraft Playing Cards	3S	3.50
1974 Fleer Hall of Fame	24	1.00
1975 Fleer Hall of Fame	18	.50
1977 Touchdown Club	25	1.50
1989 Goal Line Hall of Fame	71	2.50
1992 Packers Hall of Fame	42	.75
1993 Packers Archives Postcards	18	1.00
1996 Collector's Choice Packer Leaders	GB75	.15
1996 Collector's Choice Packers	GB57	.10

Henry Jordan (HOF, 1995)

Card	No.	Value
1961 Topps	45	15.00
1962 Post Cereal	7	3.50
1962 Salada Coins	14	8.00

1962 Topps, #72

Card	No.	Value
1962 Topps	72	6.50
1963 Topps	93	2.00
1964 Philadelphia	75	1.75
1964 Wheaties Stamps	31	3.00
1965 Philadelphia	77	1.50
1967 Philadelphia	78	1.50
1989 Goal Line Hall of Fame	177	2.00

Jerry Kramer

Card	No.	Value
1959 Topps	116	25.00
1961 Fleer	95	7.50
1961 Packers Lake to Lake	1	45.00
1962 Post Cereal	8	12.00
1962 Salada Coins	20	9.00
1963 Kahn's	34	25.00
1964 Philadelphia	76	5.00
1964 Wheaties Stamps	33	5.00
1967 Williams Portraits	214	15.00
1990 Packers 25th Anniversary	18	.75
1991 Packers Super Bowl I	25	.75
1992 Packers Hall of Fame	92	.50

Earl L. "Curly" Lambeau (HOF, 1963)

Card	No.	Value
1963 Stancraft Playing Cards	6S	2.00
1974 Fleer Hall of Fame	25	1.25
1975 Fleer Hall of Fame	31	.75
1985-87 Football Immortals	64	.35
1989 Goal Line Hall of Fame	163	2.00
1990 Notre Dame 200	134	.20
1992 Packers Hall of Fame	12	.50
1993 Packers Archives Postcards	10	.75

Dorsey Levens

Card	No.	Value
1990 Notre Dame 60	33	1.00
1994 Bowman	372	2.00
1994 Signature Rookies Tetrad Autographs	22	4.00
1996 Playoff Prime X's and O's	119	2.00
1996 Playoff Trophy Contenders Mini Back-to-Backs	16	20.00
1997 Action Packed Crash Course	14	5.00
1997 Collector's Edge Excalibur Marauders	7	3.00
1997 Collector's Edge Masters Super Bowl XXXI Game Ball	2	125.00
1997 Collector's Edge Masters Playoff Game Ball	13	15.00
1997 Pacific Crown Card Supials	12	3.00
1997 Pacific Philadelphia Photoengravings	13	3.00
1997 Playoff Absolute Pennants	25	10.00
1997 Playoff Absolute Reflex	2	30.00
1997 Playoff 1st & 10 Hot Pursuit	2	20.00

1994 Signature Rookies, #22

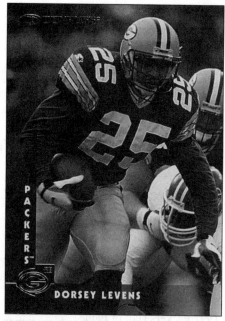

1997 Donruss, #153

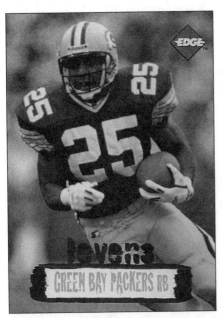

1996 Collector's Edge, #83

1996 Pro Line III, #99

1996 Collector's Edge, President's Reserve, #72

1996 Pro Line, #62

James Lofton

Card	No.	Value
1979 Topps	310	15.00
1979 Topps	407	2.75
1980 Topps	78	4.00
1981 Topps	430	3.50
1982 Topps	364	1.75

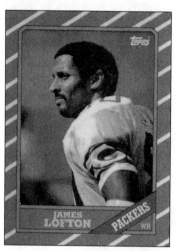

1986 Topps

1984 Topps, #272

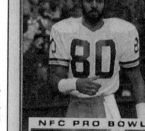

1983 Topps, #83

1982 Topps, #364

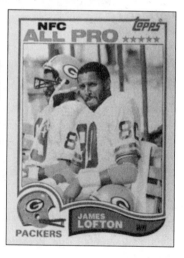

1983 Packers Police	80	4.00
1983 Topps	83	1.00
1984 Topps	272	1.50
1985 Packers Police	19	2.50
1986 DairyPak Cartons	17	5.00
1986 Packers Police	80	1.50
1991 Pro Line Portraits Autographs	31	30.00
1992 Action Packed 24k Gold	5	15.00

1982 Topps In Action, #365

1979 Topps, #310

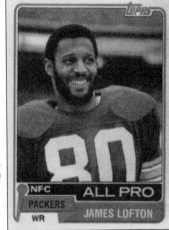

1981 Topps, #430

1981 Topps Super Action, #361

Vince Lombardi (HOF, 1971)

Card	No.	Value
1957 Giants Team Issue	22	50.00
1964 Philadelphia	84	24.00
1965 Philadelphia	84	12.00
1974 Fleer Hall of Fame	27	2.00
1975 Fleer Hall of Fame	32	.75
1985-87 Football Immortals	71	1.00
1989 Goal Line Hall of Fame	75	3.00
1990 Packers 25th Anniversary	24	1.25
1990 Pro Set	NNO	50.00
1991 Homers	1	2.00
1991 NFL Experience	3	.50
1991 Packers Super Bowl I	41	1.25
1992 Packers Hall of Fame	105	.75
1994 Ted Williams Card Co. Auckland Collection	2	7.00
1994 Ted Williams Card Co. NFL Football	67	.60
1996 Collector's Choice Packers	GB54	.50

Larry McCarren (radio voice of the Packers)

Card	No.	Value
1976 Topps	428	1.00
1977 Topps	22	.50
1978 Topps	407	.35

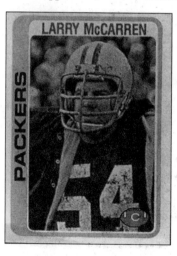

1978
Topps,
#407

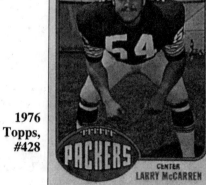

1976
Topps,
#428

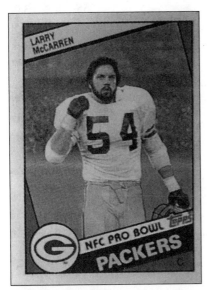

1984 Topps, #274

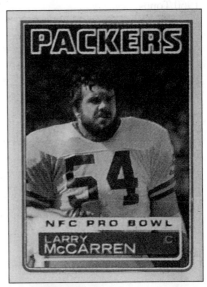

1983 Topps, #84

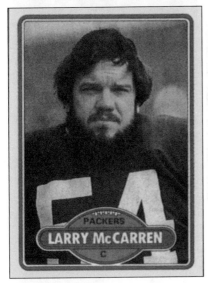

1980 Topps, #183

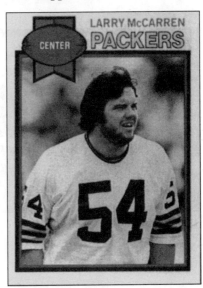

1979 Topps, #501

Max McGee *(radio voice of the Packers)*

Card	No.	Value
1959 Topps	4	20.00
1960 Topps	55	3.00
1961 Fleer	93	3.50
1961 Packers Lake to Lake	17	40.00
1961 Topps	42	2.00
1962 Post Cereal	9	3.50
1962 Salada Coins	19	7.50
1962 Topps	67	7.50
1962 Topps Bucks	36	4.50
1967 Williams Portraits	216	8.00
1990 Packers 25th Anniversary	26	.35
1990 Packers 25th Anniversary	35	.50
1991 Packers Super Bowl I	26	.50
1992 Packers Hall of Fame	87	.30

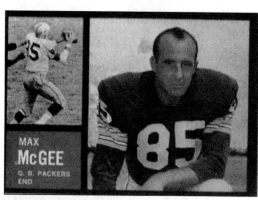

1962 Topps, #67

1960 Topps, #55

Johnny "Blood" McNally (HOF, 1963)

Card	No.	Value
1934 Diamond Matchbooks	73	30.00
1963 Stancraft Playing Cards	2C	2.00
1974 Fleer Hall of Fame	33	1.00
1975 Fleer Hall of Fame	13	.35
1989 Goal Line Hall of Fame	79	2.00
1992 Packers Hall of Fame	5	.50

Mike Michalske (HOF, 1964)

Card	No.	Value
1975 Fleer Hall of Fame	56	.35
1977 Touchdown Club	5	.75
1985-87 Football Immortals	82	.35
1989 Goal Line Hall of Fame	109	2.00
1992 Packers Hall of Fame	3	.50

Ray Nitschke (HOF, 1978)

Card	No.	Value
1961 Packers Lake to Lake	19	60.00
1963 Kahn's	48	35.00
1963 Topps	96	80.00
1965 Philadelphia	79	15.00
1966 Philadelphia	87	10.00
1967 Philadelphia	79	6.00
1967 Williams Portraits	217	18.00
1968 Topps	157	5.00
1969 Packers Tasco Prints	5	20.00
1969 Topps	55	5.00
1970 Clark Oil/Volpe Green Bay Packers	6	10.00
1970 Clark Volpe	36	15.00
1970 Topps	55	4.00
1971 Topps	133	4.50

1972 NFLPA Wonderful World Stamps	146	2.50
1972 Packers Team Issue	30	10.00
1989 Goal Line Hall of Fame	55	3.00
1990 Illinois Centennial	3	1.50
1990 Packers 25th Anniversary	7	1.00
1991 Packers Super Bowl I	43	1.00
1992 Packers Hall of Fame	107	.50
1993 Packers Archives Postcards	14	1.00
1994 Signature Rookies Gold Standard Hall of Fame	HOF18	15.00
1994 Ted Williams Card Co. Instant Replays	8	3.00
1995 Collector's Edge TimeWarp	3	20.00
1995 Collector's Edge TimeWarp Jumbos	5	10.00
1995 Collector's Edge TimeWarp Jumbos	6	10.00

Jim Ringo (HOF, 1981)

Card	*No.*	*Value*
1955 Bowman	70	35.00
1958 Topps	103	8.00
1959 Topps	75	5.00
1960 Topps	57	5.50
1961 Fleer	96	6.50
1961 Packers Lake to Lake	28	7.50
1961 Topps	44	4.25
1962 Post Cereal	11	6.00
1962 Salada Coins	22	15.00
1962 Topps	68	15.00
1963 Kahn's	66	25.00
1963 Topps	91	4.75
1964 Kahn's	36	25.00
1964 Philadelphia	78	4.00
1964 Wheaties Stamps	56	5.00
1965 Philadelphia	138	4.00
1966 Philadelphia	141	3.50
1967 Williams Portraits	379	15.00
1989 Goal Line Hall of Fame	56	2.00
1992 Packers Hall of Fame	50	.50
1993 Packers Archives Postcards	11	.75

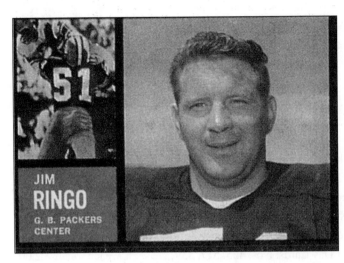

1962 Topps, #68

1960 Topps, #57

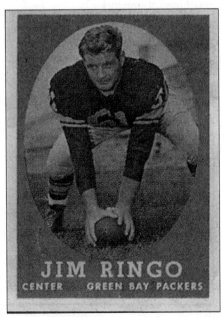

1958 Topps, #103

Eugene Robinson

Card	No.	Value
1987 Ace Fact Pack Seattle Seahawks	15	5.00
1987 Seahawks GTE	16	2.00
1987 Seahawks Snyder's/Franz	9	7.00
1989 Pro Set	401	.20
1989 Topps	191	.25
1991 Pro Line Portraits Autographs	202	6.00
1992 Breyers Bookmarks	23	1.50
1992 Pacific Picks The Pros	18	1.00
1993 McDonald's GameDay	80	1.00
1993 Stadium Club First Day Cards	141	2.00
1994 Collector's Choice Gold	168	2.00
1994 Stadium Club First Day Cards, Nos. 425, 517, 559	each	2.00
1994 Upper Deck Electric Gold	236	3.00
1995 Finest Refractors	69	3.00
1996 Finest Refractors	89	3.00
1997 Finest Refractors	67	3.00

Sterling Sharpe

Card	No.	Value
1989 Packers Police	10	2.00
1989 Score Supplemental	333	6.00
1989 Topps	379	1.50
1990 Packers Police	12	1.00
1990 Score Hot Card	10	3.00
1991 Action Packed 24k Gold	18G	20.00
1991 Pinnacle Promo Panels	9	8.00
1992 Action Packed 24k Gold	14	30.00
1992 NewSport	27	8.00
1992 Pro Line Portraits Autographs	338	20.00
1993 Action Packed All-Madden 24k Gold	9	30.00
1993 Action Packed Monday Night Football Mint	39	100.00
1993 Action Packed 24k Gold	30	30.00

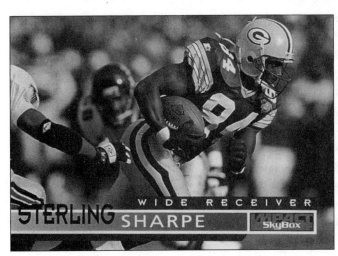

1995 SkyBox, #55

1994 Collector's Choice Gold	217	8.00
1994 Collector's Edge Excalibur Knights-NFL	6	4.00
1994 Collector's Edge F/X	7	6.00
1994 Finest Refractors	31	8.00
1994 Fleer Scoring Machines	17	5.00
1994 Images All-Pro	12	7.00
1994 Pacific Gems of the Crown	30	4.00
1994 Pinnacle Team Pinnacle	6	10.00
1994 Pinnacle/Sportflics Super Bowl	3	25.00
1994 Playoff Contenders Back-To-Backs	3	125.00
1994 Playoff Contenders Throwbacks	11	8.00
1994 Playoff Headliners Redemption	3	3.00
1994 Press Pass SB Photo Board	1	10.00
1994 Pro Line Live Autographs	49	50.00
1994 Pro Line Live MVP Sweepstakes	10	8.00
1994 Pro Set National Promos	3	5.00
1994 Score Dream Team	13	8.00
1994 Select Canton Bound	2	10.00
1994 SkyBox Revolution	8	8.00
1994 SkyBox SkyTech Stars	5	4.00
1994 Sportflics Head-To-Head	8	7.00
1994 Stadium Club First Day Cards, Nos. 108, 523	each	5.00
1994 Stadium Club First Day Cards, Nos. 240, 595	each	10.00
1994 Stadium Club Ring Leaders	7	4.00
1994 Ultra Touchdown Kings	6	6.00
1994 Upper Deck Electric Gold	280	8.00
1994 Upper Deck Hobby Predictor	8	3.00
1994 Upper Deck Retail Predictor	22	3.00
1994 Wild Card Superchrome	138	4.50
1995 Collector's Edge Excalibur 22k Gold	13	20.00
1995 Finest Fan Favorite	8	6.00
1995 Fleer Aerial Attack	6	3.00
1995 NFLPA Super Bowl Party Giveaways	9	10.00
1995 Topps 100/300 Boosters	19	3.00
1995 Upper Deck GTE Phone Cards NFC	13	4.00
1995 Zenith Z-Team	11	10.00

Bart Starr (HOF, 1977)

Card	No.	Value
1957 Topps	119	400.00
1958 Topps	66	95.00
1959 Topps	23	55.00
1960 Topps	51	40.00
1961 Fleer	88	50.00
1961 Packers Lake to Lake	18	85.00
1961 Topps	39	40.00
1962 Post Cereal	12	20.00
1962 Salada Coins	18	30.00
1962 Topps	63	70.00
1962 Topps Bucks	2	25.00
1963 Kahn's	78	50.00
1963 Topps	86	40.00
1964 Kahn's	43	50.00
1964 Philadelphia	79	40.00

1971 Topps, #200

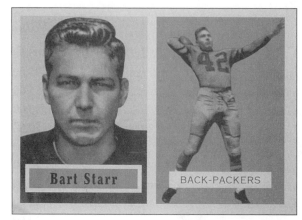

1994 Topps Archives 1957, #119

1962 Topps, #63

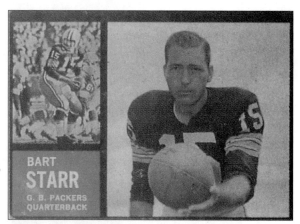

1968 Topps, #1

1969 Topps, #215

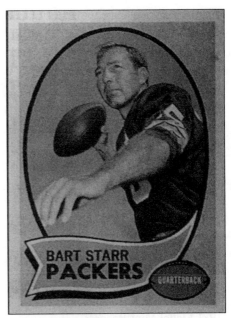

1970 Topps, #30

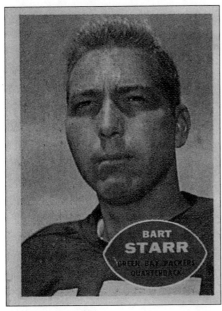

1962 Topps, #51

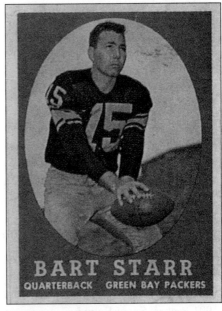

1958 Topps, #66

1964 Wheaties Stamps	64	15.00
1965 Philadelphia	81	25.00
1966 Philadelphia	88	25.00
1967 Philadelphia	82	20.00
1967 Williams Portraits	221	25.00
1968 American Oil Sweepstakes, 12a or 12b	each	6.00
1968 Topps	1	35.00
1968 Topps Posters	4	5.00
1969 Glendale Stamps	131	10.00
1969 Packers Tasco Prints	6	25.00
1969 Topps	215	25.00
1969 Topps Four In Ones	31	6.00
1970 Topps	30	20.00
1970 Topps Super Glossy	9	22.00
1970 Topps Supers	3	16.00
1971 Bazooka	21	16.00
1971 Mattel Mini-Records	17	30.00
1971 Topps	200	22.00
1971 Topps Game Cards	50	6.00
1971 Topps Pin-Ups	10	5.00
1972 NFLPA Wonderful World Stamps	150	9.00
1972 Packers Team Issue	35	12.00
1972 Packers Team Issue	45	12.00
1972 Sunoco Stamps	225	3.50
1978 Fleer Team Action	57	2.25
1979 Fleer Team Action	58	2.00
1980 Fleer Team Action	58	1.75
1983 Packers Police	xxO	4.00
1985-87 Football Immortals	108	1.25
1989 Goal Line Hall of Fame	170	6.00
1989 TV-4NFL Quarterbacks	11	1.25
1990 Packers 25th Anniversary, Nos. 2, 32	each	2.00
1991 Action Packed Whizzer White Greats	1	15.00
1991 Homers	6	3.00
1991 Packers Super Bowl I	16	1.00
1991 Packers Super Bowl I	28	1.50

Card	No.	Value
1991 Packers Super Bowl I	45	1.25
1991 Quarterback Legends	38	1.50
1991 Quarterback Legends	49	1.00
1992 Packers Hall of Fame	97	1.00
1992 Stadium Club QB Legends	2	4.00
1993 Quarterback Legends	39	1.00
1994 Ted Williams Card Co. Auckland Collection	5	7.00
1994 Ted Williams Card Co. Instant Replays	6	6.00
1994 Topps Archives 1957	119	4.00
1995 Tombstone Pizza	10	2.00
1995 Tombstone Pizza Autographs	10	30.00

Jim Taylor (HOF, 1976)

Card	No.	Value
1959 Topps	155	17.00
1960 Topps	52	8.00
1961 Fleer	89	30.00
1961 Packers Lake to Lake	13	10.00
1961 Topps	41	24.00

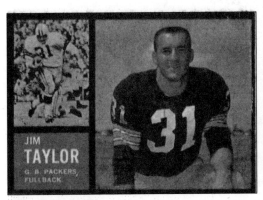

1962 Topps, #66

1960 Topps, #52

1961 Topps CFL	57	7.50
1962 Post Cereal	13	12.00
1962 Salada Coins	13	20.00
1962 Topps	66	30.00
1962 Topps Bucks	30	12.00
1963 Kahn's	83	40.00
1963 Stancraft Playing Cards	8D	3.00
1963 Topps	87	16.00
1964 Kahn's	45	30.00
1964 Philadelphia	80	15.00
1964 Wheaties Stamps	65	6.00
1965 Philadelphia	82	14.00
1966 Philadelphia	89	13.00
1967 Williams Portraits	314	20.00
1968 Topps	160	10.00
1976 Fleer Team Action	57	7.50
1981 TCMA Greats	13	1.00
1989 Goal Line Hall of Fame	145	3.00
1990 Packers 25th Anniversary	9	1.25
1990 Packers 25th Anniversary	33	.75
1992 Packers Hall of Fame	14	.75

Fred "Fuzzy" Thurston

Card	_No._	_Value_
1961 Packers Lake to Lake	22	30.00
1962 Post Cereal	14	3.50
1962 Topps	69	15.00
1963 Kahn's	85	25.00
1963 Topps	90	3.00
1967 Williams Portraits	222	7.00
1990 Packers 25th Anniversary	27	.50
1991 Packers Super Bowl I	29	.50
1992 Packers Hall of Fame	102	.20
1993 Packers Archives Postcards	15	.75

1962 Topps, #69

Reggie White

Card	No.	Value
1984 Topps USFL	58	90.00
1985 Topps USFL	75	30.00
1986 Eagles Police	2	3.50
1986 McDonald's Philadelphia Eagles	91	4.00
1986 Topps	275	12.00
1987 Eagles Police	12	16.00
1987 Topps	301	3.00
1988 Eagles Police	12	10.00
1988 Pro Set Test	4	25.00
1989 Eagles Daily News	22	6.00
1989 Eagles Smokey	92	14.00
1989 Smokey Eagles	92	12.00
1990 Eagles Police	12	8.00
1991 Action Packed NFLPA Awards	4	6.00
1991 Action Packed 24k Gold	35G	30.00
1991 Pacific Picks the Pros Silver	16	4.00
1991 Pacific Picks The Pros	16	6.00
1992 Action Packed NFLPA Mackey Awards	2	65.00

1992 Action Packed 24k Gold	32	30.00
1992 Action Packed 24K NFLPA MDA Awards	3	25.00
1992 Fleer Team Leaders	10	8.00
1992 NewSport	32	10.00
1992 Pacific Picks The Pros	12	3.00
1992 Pinnacle Team Pinnacle	11	10.00
1992 Score Dream Team	11	6.00
1992 Upper Deck Pro Bowl	7	4.00
1993 Action Packed All-Madden 24k Gold	12	25.00
1993 Action Packed Monday Night Football Mint	40	40.00
1993 Action Packed 24k Gold	72	30.00
1993 Fleer Fruit of the Loom	10	4.00
1993 Pacific Picks the Pros Gold	12	6.00
1993 Pinnacle Team Pinnacle	8	10.00
1993 Playoff Club	5	4.00
1993 Sp All-Pro	14	6.00
1993 Stadium Club First Day Cards	247	5.00
1993 Stadium Club First Day Cards	350	5.00
1993 Ultra Stars	9	10.00
1994 Action Packed All-Madden 24k Gold	16	75.00
1994 Collector's Choice Gold	237	4.00
1994 Finest Refractors	92	10.00
1994 Fleer Living Legends	6	5.00
1994 Images All-Pro	13	7.00
1994 Pinnacle Team Pinnacle	9	10.00
1994 Playoff Contenders Back-To-Backs	21	30.00
1994 Press Pass SB Photo Board	1	10.00
1994 Select Canton Bound	7	10.00
1994 SkyBox SkyTech Stars	15	4.00
1994 Sp All-Pro Holoview Die-Cuts	14	30.00
1994 Sp All-Pro Holoviews	14	4.00
1994 Sportflics Head-To-Head	6	25.00
1994 Stadium Club First Day Cards	480	5.00
1994 Stadium Club First Day Cards	629	5.00
1994 Stadium Club Ring Leaders	9	4.00
1994 Upper Deck Electric Gold	310	6.00

1995 SP, #PB14

1995 SP, #165

1995 Action Packed, #42

1995 Score Summit Edition, #139

1995 Flair, #78

1995 Stadium Club, #629

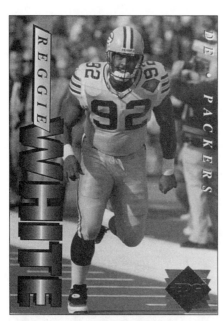

1995 Collector's Edge, #75

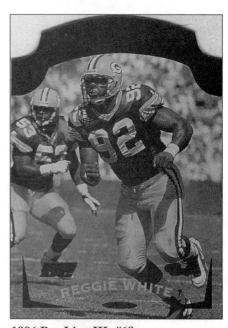

1996 Pro Line III, #68

1995 Prime Playoff, #2

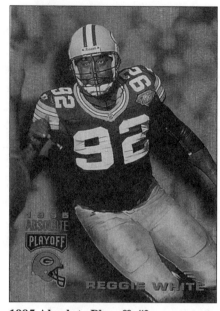

1995 Absolute Playoff, #2

1995 Pacific Crown Collection, #PB19

1995 Topps Members Only, #25

1996 Pro Line, #199

1984 Topps USFL, #58

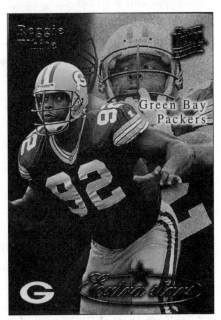

1995 Fleer Ultra, #491

Card	No.	Value
1997 Playoff Absolute Playoff Honors	PF08	125.00
1997 Playoff Absolute Reflex	6	60.00
1997 Playoff 1st & 10 Hot Pursuit	6	40.00
1997 Pro Line DC I Perennial/Future All-Pros	AP6	15.00
1997 Pro Line DC I Road to the Super Bowl	SB10	10.00
1997 Pro Line Rivalries	R5	20.00
1997 Spx Holofame	10	10.00
1997 Topps Gallery of Heroes	GH13	12.00
1997 Topps Gallery Peter Max	PM6	4.00
1997 Topps Gallery Photo Gallery	PG14	3.00
1997 Topps Hall Bound	HB4	3.00
1997 Topps Mystery Finest	M16	3.00
1997 Topps Stars Pro Bowl Stars	PB22	10.00
1997 Upper Deck Black Diamond	173	4.00
1997 Upper Deck Game Jersey	GM6	200.00

Willie Wood (HOF, 1989)

Card	*No.*	*Value*
1961 Packers Lake to Lake	36	12.00
1963 Kahn's	91	25.00
1963 Topps	95	27.00
1964 Philadelphia	82	8.00
1965 Philadelphia	83	8.00
1966 Philadelphia	90	4.50
1967 Philadelphia	83	5.00
1967 Williams Portraits	223	18.00
1969 Glendale Stamps	132	1.50
1969 Packers Tasco Prints	7	15.00
1969 Topps	168	3.50
1970 Clark Oil/Volpe Green Bay Packers	9	8.00
1970 Clark Volpe	39	10.00
1970 Topps	261	3.00
1970 Topps Super Glossy	10	7.00
1971 Topps	55	2.50
1971 Topps Game Cards	22	3.00

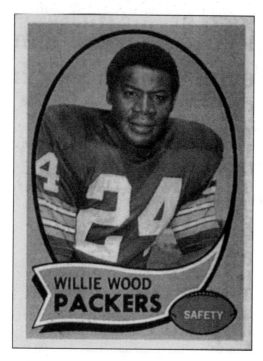

1970 Topps, #261

Most Career Touchdown Passes	Most Career Passes Caught
1. Brett Favre, 177 touchdowns 2. Bart Starr, 152 3. Lynn Dickey, 133 4. Tobin Rote, 89 5. Arnie Herber, 64	1. Sterling Sharpe, 595 2. James Lofton, 530 3. Don Hutson, 488 4. Boyd Dowler, 448 5. Max McGee, 345

Miscellaneous Packers Cards

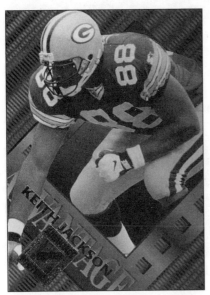

1996 Collector's Edge Advantage, #60

1996 Playoff Illusions, #103

1997 Donruss, #113

1996 Playoff Illusions, #43

1996 Pinnacle Summit, #169

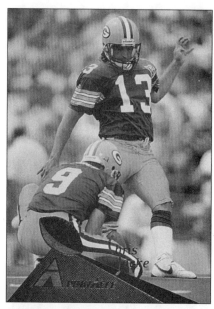

1994 Pinnacle, #174

1994 Bowman, #41

1994 Fleer GameDay, #150

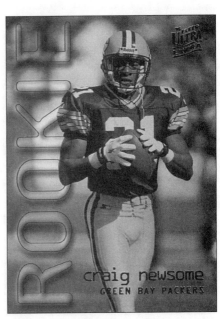

1994 Bowman, #15

1994 Fleer GameDay, #153

1994 Fleer Ultra, #397

1995 Fleer Ultra Extra, #434

1996 Topps Stadium Club, #105

1996 SP, #37

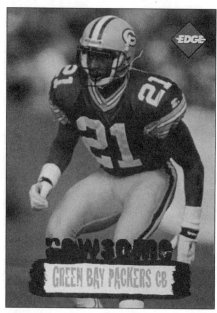

1996 Collector's Edge, #84

1994 Fleer GameDay, #149

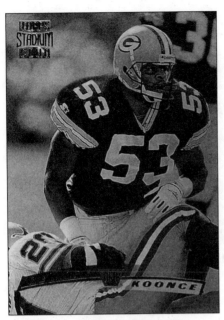

1996 Topps Stadium Club, #27

1994 Fleer Ultra, #394

1995 Fleer Metal, #72

1994 Fleer GameDay, #148

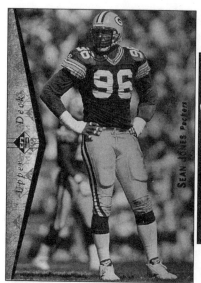

1995 SP, #53

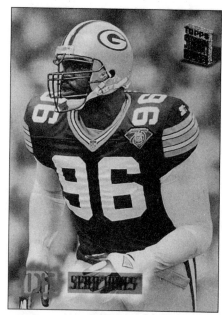

1995 Flair, #76

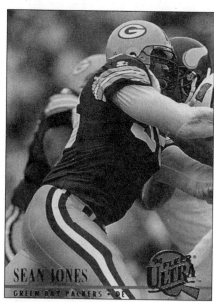

1994 Fleer Ultra, #393

1994 Topps Stadium Club, #307

1994 SP, #166

1996 Playoff Illusions, #36

1996 SkyBox Premium, #62

1996 Pinnacle, #95

1996 Topps Stadium Club, #89

1996 SP, #34

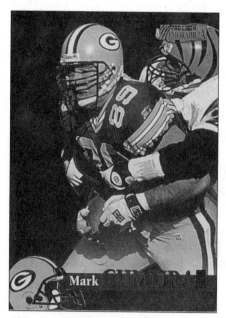

1996 Pro Line II, #58

1997 Pro Line III, #86

1997 Donruss, #109

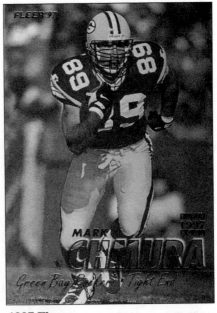

1997 Fleer

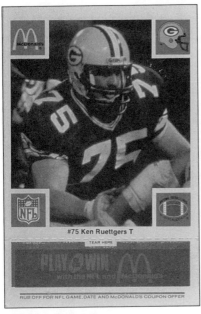

1986 McDonald's

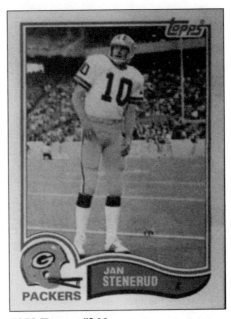

1982 Topps, #366

1982 Topps, #355

1980 Topps, #127

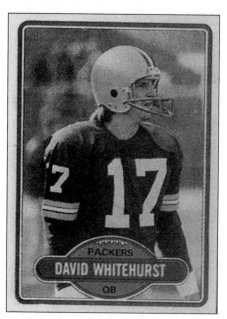

1980 Topps, #367

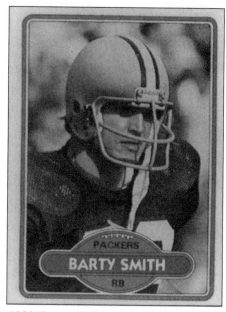

1980 Topps, #228

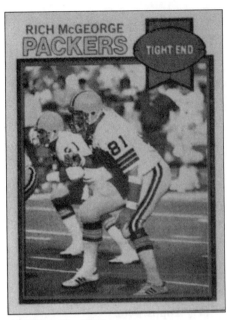

1979 Topps, #243

1979 Topps, #97

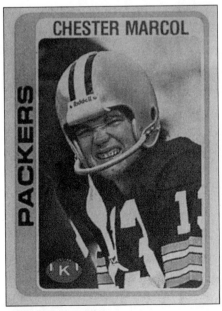

1978 Topps, #271

1976 Topps, #41

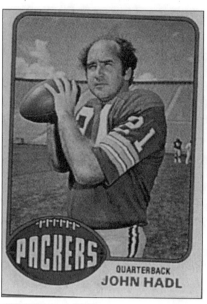

1976 Topps, #222

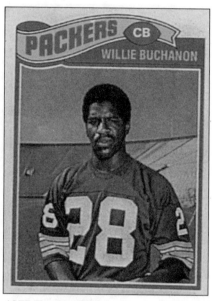

1977 Topps, #402

1977 Topps, #133

1974 Topps, #90

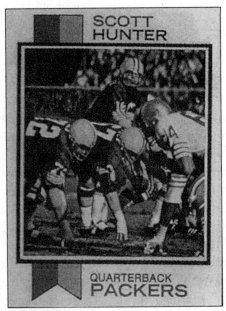

1973 Topps, #66

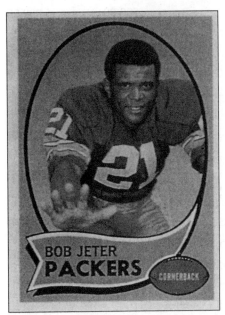

1970 Topps, #182

1973 Topps, #399

Chapter 38

Trophies and Awards

Trophies and awards are difficult to find and valuable. Most were presented annually. Any trophy or award that was presented by the NFL will be very valuable. Some local and state award will make an excellent addition to a Packers fans collection. Generally, the older the trophy or award, the more valuable. Always try to obtain as much information about the trophy or award as possible. Many of the newer ones have duplicate or samples made. Most trophies or awards stay in a football player's or coach's family, making them difficult for the collector to obtain. College awards and trophies can also be very valuable, depending on whether they are national or from the school. The two categories for prices are national awards and trophies and local and state awards and trophies. If a player or coach is in the NFL Hall of Fame, the price increases significantly.

Year		*Price Range*
1930s	500.00	5,000.00
1940s	400.00	4,000.00
1950s	350.00	3,500.00
1960s	250.00	3,000.00
1970s	125.00	1,000.00
1980s	100.00	750.00
1990s	250.00	2,500.00

Most Pass Receiving Yards in Game

1. Bill Howton vs. Los Angeles Rams, Oct. 21, 1956, 257 yards
2. Don Hutson vs. Brooklyn, Nov. 21, 1943, 237
3. Don Beebe vs. San Francisco, Oct. 14, 1996, 220
4. Don Hutson vs. Cleveland Rams, Oct. 18, 1942, 209
5. Don Hutson vs. Chicago Cardinals, Nov. 1, 1942, 207

Chapter 39

Video Films and Tapes

Old Packers game films are hard to locate and valuable. Otto Stiller recorded many early games that were lost due to damage in storage. Film is destroyed easily by heat; the chemicals in old films cause deterioration if they are not stored in the proper temperature and humidity. Early game films from the 1940s and 1950s can bring up to several hundred each! In the late 1950s and early 1960s, 8mm film became popular. It was easy to use and many people started doing home movies. Any home movies of 1960s Packers games are valuable today. A large number of game highlight films became available. These highlight films have some value, but they have nowhere near the price of complete game films. In the late 1970s, video recorders (VCRs) become available, making game films much easier to obtain. The quality and completeness of a game film are important factors in assessing its price. Complete Championship and Super Bowl films are valuable and difficult to find.

Years	_Price Range_	
1920s	100.00	1,000.00+
1930s	100.00	750.00+
1940s	100.00	500.00+
1950s	75.00	300.00+
1960s	75.00	500.00+
1970s	50.00	150.00+
1980s	15.00	75.00
1990s	10.00	35.00

Most Pass Receiving Yards in a Season

1. Robert Brooks, 1,497 yards
2. Sterling Sharpe, 1,461
3. Sterling Sharpe, 1,423
4. James Lofton, 1,361
5. James Lofton, 1,300

Chapter 40

Yearbooks/Salute to the Packers

The Packers have the longest continuously printed yearbooks in the NFL. The first yearbook was published in 1960. Because of the limited number of early yearbooks available, completing a set is both challenging and rewarding. A complete set can be worth several thousand dollars in top condition. The cover is very important and determines most of a yearbook's price, along with other condition factors such as tears, stains, writing, creases and fading. Yearbooks have a section in the back to score the games each week. If a yearbook is scored, it takes away about 10% to 25% of the price. A scored yearbook is not considered damaged because the scoring was meant to be done.

The most difficult post 1960s yearbook to obtain is the 1977. The yearbook went through a transition in ownership during 1977 and this may account for the difficulty in finding them. Yearbooks are

1962 Packers Yearbook ($75-$200).

gaining in popularity because of the large number of Hall of Famers on the covers and the increase in value of a set in recent years.

Salute to the Packer magazines were similar to the Packer yearbooks. They were published annually during the glory years from 1961-1968, except 1963 when no issues were printed. They are full of exellent photographs and articles. The most difficult issue to obtain is the 1965 version. Fewer were printed and they are the most valuable. Packer Salutes make an excellent addition to any 1960s collection.

The three categories of condition are Poor-Fair, Good-Very Good and Excellent or better. Poor to Fair is complete, but it will have major damage to the cover and/or the inside such as tears, heavy creases, obvious staining, a loose cover, severe fading and writing. Good to Very Good is average condition, showing normal wear such as light creases, very small tears or light staining. Excellent or better condition will appear almost new inside and out.

Store your yearbooks in individual bags or envelopes and keep them in a clean, dry area. Yearbooks that are incomplete or missing the cover have very little value. A complete set of yearbooks from 1960 to the present, depending on condition, would run from $700 to more than $2,000.

Year		*Price Range*
1960	100.00	300.00+
1961	100.00	250.00+
1962	75.00	200.00
1963	60.00	175.00
1964	50.00	125.00
1965	50.00	125.00
1966	45.00	110.00
1967	45.00	110.00
1968	40.00	100.00
1969	15.00	45.00
1970	12.00	40.00
1971	12.00	40.00
1972	12.00	40.00
1973	12.00	40.00
1974	10.00	35.00
1975	12.00	40.00
1976	10.00	35.00
1977	25.00	60.00
1978	8.00	25.00
1979	8.00	25.00
1980	8.00	25.00
1981	7.00	20.00
1982	7.00	20.00
1983	7.00	20.00
1984	7.00	20.00
1985	5.00	15.00

1986	5.00	15.00
1987	5.00	15.00
1988	5.00	15.00
1989	5.00	15.00
1990	5.00	15.00
1991	5.00	15.00
1992	8.00	25.00
1993	8.00	25.00
1994	8.00	25.00
1995	8.00	25.00
1996	8.00	25.00
1997	8.00	12.00

Salute to the Packers

1961	45.00	95.00
1962	45.00	95.00
1964	40.00	80.00
1965	60.00	125.00
1966	50.00	100.00
1967	50.00	100.00
1968	50.00	100.00

1961 Packers Yearbook ($100-$250+).

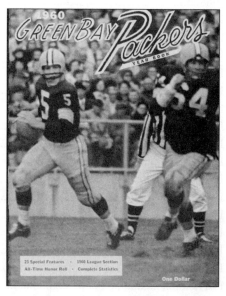

1960 Packers Yearbook ($100-$300+).

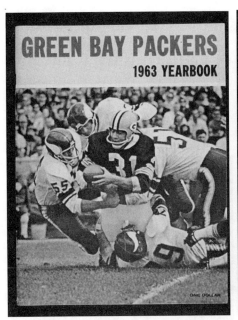

1963 Packers Yearbook ($60-$175).

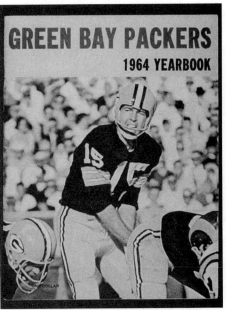

1964 Packers Yearbook ($50-$125).

1965 Packers Yearbook ($50-$125).

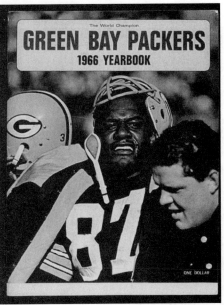

1966 Packers Yearbook ($45-$110).

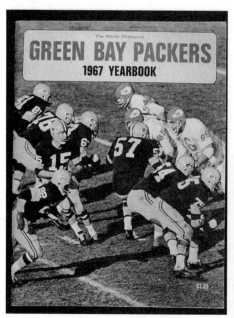

1967 Packers Yearbook ($45-$110).

1968 Packers Yearbook ($40-$100).

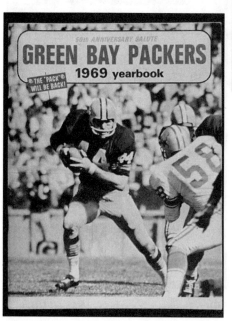

1969 Packers Yearbook ($15-$45).

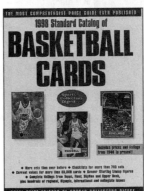

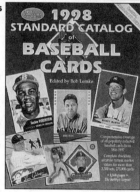

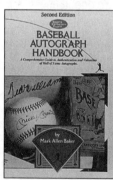